"Wendy is one of the most clear, compass̲ ̲ ̲ ̲ ̲ ̲ ̲ ̲ ̲ ̲ ̲
I know. For years, she has been my go-to healer when I've needed a second look at my own energy. As an empath myself, I found Wendy's book deeply insightful, and I'm sure it's destined to help many people. Thank you, Wendy, for sharing your gifts with the world!"

— **Jeffrey Allen**, energy healer, teacher, and Mindvalley author and speaker

"A much-needed guide for navigating intuitive sensitivity, *Becoming an Empowered Empath* shows you how to reclaim your inner power without being overwhelmed by it. Wendy De Rosa speaks from the heart, faithfully leading us into the wisdom, healing, and joy of an insightful life."

— **Kim Chestney**, author of *Radical Intuition: A Revolutionary Guide to Using Your Inner Power*

"Wendy De Rosa is a real-deal teacher with insights that are both practical and profound. If you've struggled with your empathic ability and found it to be a challenge, Wendy will help you turn it into one of your greatest blessings."

— **Stephen Dinan**, CEO, The Shift Network

"Reading Wendy De Rosa's book made me feel like she had crawled inside my head and begun writing from that space. Being an intuitive empath for as long as I can remember, I had always felt that no one understood me. Decades of therapy, self-help books and programs, and meditation fixed most of my brokenness, but *Becoming an Empowered Empath* feels like the final missing piece. I had so many aha moments of 'finally, someone who understands!' If you're an empath, get out a highlighter — you're going to need it."

— **Michelle S. Fondin**, author of *Chakra Healing for Vibrant Energy* and *The Wheel of Healing with Ayurveda*

"Wendy De Rosa understands the true plight of the empath. Her step-by-step, easy-to-read book offers a brilliant pathway for empaths to reignite their spark, reclaim their personal power, and recover lost aspects of Soul. It is a must-read for all who crave a deeper connection with themselves and with the world around them and who desire to step onto the path of energetic mastery. Think of it as a guide to thriving — more than just a book."

— **Corin Grillo**, author of *The Angel Experiment:*
A 21-Day Magical Adventure to Heal Your Life

"Wendy offers all the tools empaths need to stand in their power and use their intuitive gifts as a force for good in the world."

— **Lee Harris**, author of *Energy Speaks*
and creator of the Empaths vs. Narcissists online course

"*Becoming an Empowered Empath* is the precious guidebook we so urgently need right now in order to navigate our high-stakes world with ease — by learning to heal from the traumas of our past and establishing energetic boundaries. Wendy De Rosa provides a spiritual toolbox, not only for empaths but for all of us looking to balance the body and the Soul so that we may find a deeper awareness of Self, connect with our inner light, and heal our energy centers. In a world that doesn't always value sensitivity, Wendy gives us the courage to take back our empathic power."

— **Bill Philipps**, author of *Expect the Unexpected:*
Bringing Peace, Healing, and Hope from the Other Side
and *Signs from the Other Side: Opening to the Spirit World*

"*Becoming an Empowered Empath* is a lifeline for anyone who has found themselves taking on the energy of others. Wendy De Rosa shows us what we can do to help maintain our energetic boundaries and therefore show up fully as a healing force in the world. I absolutely love Wendy's meditations, her journaling exercises, and her tools that are based on getting grounded in your lower chakras. This book has helped me, and I know it will help you, too!"

— **Corinne Zupko**, award-winning author of
From Anxiety to Love: A Radical New Approach for Letting Go
of Fear and Finding Lasting Peace

Becoming an EMPOWERED EMPATH

Becoming an
EMPOWERED
EMPATH

HOW TO CLEAR ENERGY,
SET BOUNDARIES &
EMBODY YOUR INTUITION

Wendy De Rosa

Foreword by Gabrielle Bernstein

New World Library
Novato, California

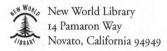

New World Library
14 Pamaron Way
Novato, California 94949

Text design by Tona Pearce Myers
Illustration on p. 41 by Saori Murphy

Library of Congress Cataloging-in-Publication Data

Names: De Rosa, Wendy, author.
Title: Becoming an empowered empath : how to clear energy, set boundaries &
    embody your intuition / Wendy De Rosa.
Description: Novato, California : New World Library, [2021] | Summary:
    "Describes the unique problems of being an empath — a person who senses
    and vividly experiences the emotions of others — and provides methods for
    setting boundaries, healing trauma, and finding inner peace"— Provided by
    publisher.
Identifiers: LCCN 2020055446 (print) | LCCN 2020055447 (ebook) | ISBN
    9781608687190 (paperback) | ISBN 9781608687206 (epub)
Subjects: LCSH: Sensitivity (Personality trait) | Intuition. | Empathy.
Classification: LCC BF698.35.S47 D42 2021 (print) | LCC BF698.35.S47
    (ebook) | DDC 155.2/32--dc23
LC record available at https://lccn.loc.gov/2020055446
LC ebook record available at https://lccn.loc.gov/2020055447

First printing, March 2021
ISBN 978-1-60868-719-0
Ebook ISBN 978-1-60868-720-6
Printed in Canada on 100% postconsumer-waste recycled paper

New World Library is proud to be a Gold Certified Environmentally Responsible Publisher. Publisher certification awarded by Green Press Initiative.

10   9   8   7   6   5   4   3   2

This book is dedicated to empaths everywhere and to the power of our human spirits to heal, grow, and evolve together — for ourselves and for generations to come.

It is also dedicated to my family, friends, students, and team at the School of Intuitive Studies, who made this book possible through their unwavering support and commitment to living their light in the world.

Contents

Foreword

In the fall of 2019, I taught a six-day intensive workshop at the Kripalu Center for Yoga & Health in Stockbridge, Massachusetts. By the second day of the program, I noticed that the energy was intense due to difficult topics that came up early in the first session. As a motivational speaker, I'd had more than a decade of experience leading large events, but intensive retreats weren't something I did often. At times I found these events to be draining. And there I was again, the second day into the program, already feeling overwhelmed by the group energy and the responsibility that goes with the work.

The third morning of the program, I woke up early to meditate and get centered. After my meditation, I headed to the faculty dining room, and as I entered, I noticed a lovely woman at the table drinking tea. Her energy drew me in, and her smile put me at ease. I sat down, and we introduced ourselves as fellow teachers at the center. Little did I know she would soon become a teacher to me.

"My name is Wendy," she said. "I'm teaching a workshop on how to stop taking on the energy of others." I smiled and replied, "Wow, I need that right now!" I went on to share what was going on with my group. I opened up to her and said I was struggling to stay centered and manage the energy of the group. "You need to practice co-regulating," she said. "You don't have to be the victim of the energy. Instead, you're here to help raise consciousness and lead by example with true sensitivity and heart."

This statement knocked my socks off! I didn't want the conversation to end, but I had to head to class. I finished my coffee, checked the time, and said, "Can we meet again tomorrow morning? I think I have more to learn from you!"

This was the beginning of my profoundly impactful relationship with Wendy De Rosa. From that day on, she has been a mentor, guide, and healer to me, in more ways than she will ever know. Wendy has taught me that I no longer have to struggle to manage my empathy and that I can use it as a force for good instead.

Wendy is precisely the spiritual mentor I would pray for you to find. By opening this book, you will receive the energetic nurturing that she has infused into every page. These practices will clear the wounds you came into this world with, as well as the wounds imprinted in your system from childhood. Releasing these blocks will reveal your greatest source of power and inner freedom.

Today, through Wendy's guidance, I am no longer a victim of the energy of the world. This book, and her wisdom, have guided me to intuitively know how to alchemize the energy of others by speaking my truth and having empathy, while staying steady in my energetic center. I know God guided me to the breakfast table that day, to crack me open to a greater sense of inner awareness and spiritual growth.

Now it's your turn.

— Gabby Bernstein, #1 *New York Times* bestselling author of *The Universe Has Your Back*

CHAPTER ONE

Your Gifts as an Empath

D o you feel other people's energy — whether they are stressed, anxious, angry, or in need? You may even sense that you absorb their energy. When you enter a room, you can pick up on the energy present, how people are feeling, or what might be happening. You're likely sensitive to what's occurring around you — including injustice, political divisions, the effects of climate change, the danger of extinction of animals, and more — and to the pain of others in your community and in our world. You also sense the powerful energies that are emerging to bring about change.

This is the experience of living as an empath, a person who is highly sensitive and, as a result, feels and absorbs other people's energy, emotions, and even physical symptoms. Empaths experience their world through their intuition and a felt sense of people and situations. They might not be able to define why they feel the way they do, but they sense that they are impacted by other people's energy.

Empathy has become a popular topic recently, much of it inspired by the work of researcher and author Brené Brown. Empathy is a person's capacity to understand or relate to what another person is experiencing. Brown describes empathy as a skill that can bring people together and make them feel included.

While it is natural to feel the energy around you and to connect with other people's emotions, problems arise when you absorb these energies or take on these emotions as your own. You can likely recall an experience when you moved from attentive listening (hearing how someone is feeling about an experience) to taking on someone else's experience (feeling it as if it were happening to you). People generally love talking to empaths because of this. They feel so much better and describe themselves as "relieved" afterward. That's because the empath in their life just took on dealing with their problems for them!

Problems arise from being *overly* empathic. This experience of taking on the feelings and experiences of another person as your own can be described as "merging" with another person. It is helpful to imagine empathic nature on a spectrum: on one end, empathy and understanding operate with detachment, and on the other, being empathic and intuitive leads to merging.

For empaths, merging occurs because they are not fully present, or "inhabiting," their own energy body — particularly the lower body and lower chakras, energetic centers within the body. (When I refer to "energy" or "energy body," I am referring to the energetic field that is in and around your physical body. In the next chapter, we'll discuss in detail the subtle energy body and the chakras and how they relate to our empathic intuition.) Not being fully present in your lower body area leaves a vacancy for other people's energy to take over. Some of the physical and emotional symptoms of taking on other people's energy include stress, agitation, depletion, and feeling overwhelmed and overstimulated. Depression, digestive issues, migraines, allergies, and other physical illnesses may also manifest. This pattern of taking on other people's energy often starts in childhood, before one learns to maintain emotional or energetic boundaries. Perhaps as a child you were told that you were "too sensitive"? (And maybe you still hear this today?) You may have learned to take on other people's energy as a way to help them or to calm them down. In fact, you likely developed this impulse to merge with others as a way to seek love and intimacy and to keep yourself safe.

Being overly empathic is common when a child is raised in a household with unclear boundaries, projected emotions, suppression of self, or no feeling of safety or belonging. Children learn to survive by prioritizing other people's needs and energy while disconnecting from their self and their own needs.

These survival and coping mechanisms take root in the first chakra area of the body and, once formed, create energetic imprints in your body that can lead to unhealthy patterns in a number of areas in your life — your health, your relationships, your work, and more. Largely unconscious, this response becomes ingrained as a default setting, influencing your worldview and how you interact with family, friends, and coworkers. You may not intend to absorb the energy around you, but your subtle energy body is responding in the only way it knows to keep you safe. In addition, Western culture often views sensitivity as a weakness or a liability, so as children we're taught to avoid, dismiss, or suppress our feelings and needs, ultimately invalidating our intuitive sense. This causes us to disconnect from ourselves and our inner guidance and creates a lack of trust in our instincts and intuition. The disconnection is not just mental, emotional, or energetic; it is spiritual as well, sometimes referred to as being disconnected from one's Soul.*

Though you may have tried different methods to heal these patterns — perhaps therapy, workshops, self-help books, or various spiritual practices — you likely found that these tools alone were not enough to shift lifelong patterns or to help you set and hold healthy boundaries.

To stop taking on other people's energy requires not just an understanding of your physical body and symptoms but also an understanding of your *energetic body*. The lower chakras are the main power centers in the energetic anatomy. They house the primary conditioning for every human being's survival imprints, coping mechanisms, personality traits, and personal power. They are responsible for how you relate to yourself, others, and the world. A "reparenting" of the lower chakras (nurturing yourself and inhabiting your energy body) will help you shift from being overly sensitive to empowered.

These lower chakras are closely tied to the empathic power of intuition, feeling, and self-expression. Throughout Western culture and history, these aspects have been subjected to collective and societal shaming. The shaming of sensitivity, vulnerability, truth, emotions, and creativity has limited the power of our true selves, causing us to suppress our true feelings, true voice, true being, and true sense of belonging.

---

* Throughout the book, I spell *Soul* and *Self* with a capital S to refer to one's higher or divine Self or Soul.

Empaths need not be victims to the world around them. I know it can seem that way when you are feeling everyone's energy, but when you feel triggered by another individual's energy, think of it as an opportunity to address the deeper layers within you that need to be seen, healed, and brought into alignment. The good news is that empaths are awakening and learning about their empathic nature so they can heal their early-life wounds and fully express their gifts.

Your gift as an empath is that you feel what's true. You are connected to the subtle and can see beneath the layers. By expanding your capacity to embody your empathic gifts, you become uniquely equipped to show others how to experience their authentic feelings and help heal the planet. This is a critical step at this time: we need empowered empaths who can give voice to what is unspoken, bring to light what is hidden, and heal what is suppressed.

In this book you will learn more about your energetic body and Soul and how to reparent the energy in your body as it relates to empathic intuition. This book will also address the misconception that empaths have to struggle with managing energy. In fact, empaths are here to help raise consciousness, leading by example with true sensitivity and heart.

With the proper framework, described in the following chapters, empaths will have the tools to transform the effects of their past and come to understand the true nature of their empathic power. You will finally be able to show up with your gifts in your relationships, work, and other parts of your life. You will find that it's possible to feel nourished and to thrive as an empowered empath. You will be able to restore your energetic boundaries and align with your true light and power. This is a most profound experience of self-love and is essential for establishing an uncompromising and loving connection with yourself, regardless of external circumstances or challenges and throughout your daily activities and interactions with others.

It is time to fully express and embody your empathic intuition and power.

How to Use the Exercises in This Book

I recommend that as you read this book, you keep a journal and write down the insights that come to you. This will help you shift your focus out of your head and into your body. (Journaling will help you track your transformation, too!) I also encourage you to engage with the journaling exercises at the ends of most of the chapters.

I have created a guided healing meditation for most chapters to support you in deepening and integrating the teachings. You can find downloadable audio or streaming video for the meditations by going to the URL listed with each one. Or you can read the meditation and guide yourself; record yourself reading the meditation out loud and then listen to your recording; or have someone read the meditation to you and act as your guide.

But first, I invite you to set an intention for what you would like to receive by learning more about your empathic nature from this book. Setting intentions is a powerful way to open to a process and steer your journey to healing and transformation. Intentions also bring to your conscious awareness opportunities for growth. Here's a short guided meditation to support you in getting clear and grounded in your intention so you can fully embody it. After the meditation, have your journal or paper handy.

....

Guided Meditation: Intention Setting

Audio version available at WendyDeRosa.com/book-meditations

....

Let's begin by taking a comfortable seat.

Close your eyes and breathe deeply into your heart. Imagine a cord strongly connecting your hips to the center of the earth and feel yourself grounded through that cord.

In the middle of your chest, your beautiful heart chakra carries a deep calling for living your truth in the world. Bring your awareness into the center of your heart and breathe deeply into the illuminating light of your Soul's essence.

Through the heart chakra, your Soul is calling you to live in alignment with your gifts. Listen deeply to the light of your heart. What is it asking of you in this life?

Breathe and listen.

Now take a moment and set an intention for what you would like to receive out of this book. What would you like to shift or support about your empathic nature?

Set this intention between your heart and the Divine.

Sense the energy in your body; feel your connection to the earth.

Take your time and sense the power of your intention. As you are ready, feel that intention vibrant and strong in the center of your heart and offer it up to the universe.

When you feel complete, you can slowly open your eyes.

JOURNALING EXERCISE

After reading or listening to the guided meditation above, take a few minutes to journal your first impressions, thoughts, and feelings from the practice. Capture your intention for what you would most like to receive from reading and working with the material in this book. Consider these questions if you need prompts:

1. What patterns are you ready to heal and release?
2. What is the change you most want to create in your life?
3. How will these practices help you?

CHAPTER TWO

Your Subtle Energy Body
and the Four Aspects of Intuition

Y ou are likely familiar with the chakra system and may even have a regular practice for working with your energy body. For those who are not yet familiar with the chakras, it is important to have a foundational understanding of them before diving deeper and exploring how empaths absorb energy.

The chakras were first written about in the ancient Hindu texts called the Vedas. The word *chakra* was derived from the Sanskrit word *cakra*, meaning "wheel" or "disk." These "wheels of energy" are power centers in your subtle body, also known as your energy body or energy field, which extends well beyond your physical body, above, below, and all around you. The chakras are located throughout and around the body, from below the feet, up through the body along the spine, and all the way up through the crown and above the head. They are called "wheels of energy" because ancient seers and even intuitives today see these energy centers as dynamic, rotating, pulsing, and spinning circles of light.

The chakras are perceived energy centers, which means that you won't see them with the naked eye, but through states of meditation you can intuit colors, imagery, sounds, tones, and vibrations associated with them. They are linked to your health and wellbeing, and they carry immense information about your existence — your characteristics, qualities, history, and way of operating in the world. When your chakras become imbalanced because of energetic imprints or blockages, you become imbalanced mentally, emotionally, physically, and spiritually.

The chakras act as portals to higher levels of consciousness and awareness. To understand the patterns in the body that impact the empath, refer to the chakra illustration on the next page, which lists the names and characteristics of each chakra. In this book, I will mostly be addressing energetic imprints held in the first three chakras.

Each chakra carries power and the history of our wounds. We can heal these wounds by releasing energy stored in the chakras and their corresponding domains in the body. The chakras relate to the organs of the body as well, so when physical ailments or health issues are present, you can clear underlying blocks in the energy system and chakras to allow more vital life-force energy to flow, which supports physical healing. In other words, "Our issues are in our tissues" (as some yoga teachers like to say). Awareness of the chakra system can help us identify what issues are stored where in our body.

When empaths are experiencing oversensitivity, it usually means that wounded energy or blocks are present in one or more of the chakras, preventing the body from operating in its state of full potentiality. The more conscious we are of the energy we are holding in our chakras, the more embodied and

THE SEVEN CHAKRAS

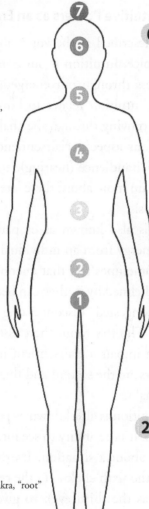

Seventh Chakra: Crown Chakra
Sanskrit name: Sahasrara chakra,
"thousand petaled" (lotus)
Location: above the top of the head
Color: white or multicolored
Areas of governance: brain, cranial nerves
Qualities: faith, spiritual connection, divine love, infinite
potential

Fifth Chakra: Throat Chakra
Sanskrit name: Vishuddha
chakra, "purification"
Location: throat
Color: blue
Areas of governance: throat,
neck, thyroid, mouth, teeth,
tongue, jaw
Qualities: speaking truth,
communication, self-
expression, intuitive
listening, discernment

Sixth Chakra: Third Eye Chakra
Sanskrit name: Ajna chakra, "to
command and perceive"
Location: center of forehead
Color: indigo
Areas of governance:
pituitary gland, pineal gland,
skull, eyes, brain, nervous
system, the senses
Qualities: higher knowing,
perception, intuition,
imagination, wisdom

Third Chakra: Solar Plexus
Chakra
Sanskrit name: Manipura
chakra, "lustrous gem"
or "jeweled city"
Location: from the navel to the
diaphragm
Color: yellow
Areas of governance:
digestive system, including
the stomach and upper
intestines; midback
and solar plexus region
Qualities: will, identity,
digestion, instincts or sense
of knowing, manifesting,
taking action

Fourth Chakra: Heart Chakra
Sanskrit name: Anahata
chakra, "unhurt,"
"unstruck," or "pure"
Location: center of chest
Color: green, pink, or gold
Areas of governance: heart,
lungs, blood, circulatory
system
Qualities: human and
spiritual love, kindness,
generosity, self-love,
compassion, joy, purpose

Second Chakra: Sacral Chakra
Sanskrit name: Svadhisthana chakra,
"seat of self" or "one's own
dwelling"
Location: pelvic bone
Color: orange
Areas of governance: sexual organs,
bladder, bowel, lower intestines
Qualities: sexuality, creativity,
emotions, empathic intuition,
femininity, sweetness, mothering

First Chakra: Root Chakra
Sanskrit name: Muladhara chakra, "root"
Location: tailbone
Color: ruby red
Area of governance: base of spine
Qualities: survival, security, safety, trust,
grounding, nurturing, strength

healthy we feel. Later in this book I will be explaining the negative energy patterns that are stored in particular chakras and how healing this energy supports the empath's ability to be both empowered and intuitive.

Your Intuitive Powers as an Empath

Intuition is often described as the voice of our Soul, but it's more than just a voice. Intuition is our Soul communicating to our consciousness through our energetic system. To take this a step further, intuition relates to how much prana, or life-force energy, is moving through the chakras.

Intuition has four aspects: clairsentience (feeling), clairvoyance (seeing), clairaudience (hearing), and claircognizance (knowing). I'll explain more about these later in the book, but here is a brief synopsis.

Clairsentience is also known as empathic intuition. It's the ability to feel energy from an individual or a collective. A clairsentient will sometimes feel that energy in their body. If they become overwhelmed by it, they can become emotionally and energetically congested, disconnecting them from their intuitive guidance. The less room there is for Self, the more this congestion can impair a clairsentient intuitive. The empathic power centers are the second and third chakras and the heart, the fourth chakra.

Clairvoyant intuition is also known as perception, psychic intuition, or visions. It's the ability to see intuitively or to have higher perceptions about a situation. It's the visionary sense that operates from the sixth chakra, in the center of your forehead (also known as the third eye), to give you heightened awareness.

Clairaudience is hearing or perceiving intuitive messages

from the higher realm. It's what happens, for example, in mediumship, which is the process of facilitating messages from the spirit world. Clairaudience is also hearing your inner child's messages, or messages from your heart, or songs, or the same message coming to you from multiple people or sources. The back side of the fifth chakra, the throat chakra, is connected to listening intuitively.

Claircognizance often describes an ability in people who get the feeling of knowing; they don't know why they know — they just know. They are people who receive kinesthetic responses to intuitive "hits" through chills, a sudden ache, or another sensation in the body. They also sometimes need to move their body for intuition to be activated. Claircognizance relates to the first, second, third, and fourth chakras. The knowing sense becomes activated in these power centers when the Soul is receiving an intuition.

The empath feels energy; however, someone who hears messages, sees images and higher insights, or knows something on a deep level without knowing why would not necessarily be an empath. On the other hand, someone could be an empath and simultaneously have other aspects of intuition activated as well.

What I've come to understand about myself is that I have all four aspects of intuition. Not knowing that throughout my earlier years, and being particularly sensitive, I was overwhelmed by the energy that was coming in from a lot of different directions. I had no modeling of how to be with the energy or with myself.

My point here is that you could be more than empathic (clairsentient). In addition to feeling energy, you could also be clairvoyant, clairaudient, claircognizant, or any combination of the four. You could also have come into this world with strong chakras that are fueling your intuitive abilities.

In this book I will talk about how these four aspects relate to an empath's experience with intuition. I'll also explain the difference between upper- and lower-body intuition and why it is important to strengthen the empathic aspect in order for the other three aspects to feel embodied and integrated.

For now, what's important to know is that doing the work in this book will help you with healing, strengthening your center, holding boundaries, and developing stronger empathic intuition, as well as with cultivating the other three aspects of intuition. I want to focus on supporting you to live as an empowered empath so you can ground into who you really are and feel whole as an intuitive being.

The work here is to clear the wounds you came into this world with and the wounds imprinted in your system in childhood so you can discover what power means for you. Imprints are life experiences or stored memories that exist in the energy system. Sometimes those imprints are good, like the feeling of being loved as a child. Sometimes the imprints are negative, like the impact of being neglected, hearing that you aren't good enough, or being told that who you are is "less than."

In later chapters, I will explain the energetic anatomy in more detail, including specific systems connected to the lower chakras. For empaths, the imprints, energetic blocks, and feelings of being overwhelmed are held specifically in the lower three chakras because they house more of our human experiences, history, and inherent patterns with which we came into this world.

Patterns stem from our belief systems, ingrained conditioning, trauma, imprints, and life experiences that were formed in this life or past lives or else passed on to us intergenerationally. What we have learned conditions us to disconnect from our innate essence and intuition. As we unlearn these patterns, we can release stagnant and blocked energy and embody ourselves fully. When you know who you are and why you are here, you can change the pattern of absorbing energy and shift into living in alignment with your true divine Self.

On this journey together, we will engage in deep guided healing to clear karma, contracts, and beliefs from lifetimes and from your lineage and to release the energetic blocks you are holding in your body. You are here to speak your truth, hold your emotional center, have empathy, and sense — but not absorb into your system — other people's energy. You will stop feeling that you're at the mercy of others' negative energy and instead activate the power of your emotional connection. You'll contribute to life by acting as a clear channel to bring spirit through you.

Your journey begins with clearing inherited negative imprinting.

Guided Meditation: Chakra Clearing
Audio version available at WendyDeRosa.com/book-meditations

This is a chakra meditation to help you orient yourself to the power centers of your body. If you are listening to this meditation, close your eyes and take some deep breaths. If you are reading it, take time to pause in between phrases.

Let's begin.

Take a comfortable seat.

Bring your awareness to your hips and your sitz bones and

imagine a tree trunk is secured to the sides of your hips, the front of your pelvis, and the back of your pelvis. This tree trunk extends deep beneath the earth's crust and sprouts its roots around the core of the earth. It represents your grounding cord. Your grounding cord is your connection to the vibration in the center of the earth that is nurturing, safe, secure, and still.

Take your time as you allow your body to settle. Breathe into a feeling of safety and security as your grounding cord holds you.

Shift your awareness now to your tailbone region, where you find a beautiful ruby-red power center. This is your root chakra, the Muladhara chakra. It is the earth element in your body and is much slower than the mind. It carries the power of safety, trust, security, belonging, innate love, and information about your culture, your physical body, and your survival on this planet. Take some deep breaths into this center, holding the power of claiming safety and trust in your body. Exhale any conscious or subconscious fears about existing on this earth. Inhale safety and trust. Exhale deep subconscious fear. Let the energy release down and out of your grounding cord.

Now move your awareness to your pelvic region. In the pelvic bowl is a beautiful, vibrant orange chakra called your sacral chakra, the Svadhisthana chakra. This is the water element in your body. It relates to the quality of going with the flow. It is sensual and in tune with the divine feminine, with the rhythms of life. It is your sexuality, your creativity, your cocreation with the Divine, birthing, and the spectrum of emotions. Trust in Self at the root chakra is the foundation for the power of trust in this, your second chakra. Breathe into relaxing and receiving your beautiful innate essence of playfulness and sweetness. Exhale and release any feelings of guilt, over-responsibility, shame, or suppressed emotions. Breathe through all you are feeling. Let your exhales be strong, and let your inhales be nourishing and loving to this area of your body.

Now bring your awareness to the solar plexus region between your navel and your diaphragm. This is your third chakra, the Manipura chakra. It is the fire element in your body and governs the digestion, assimilation, and transformation of food, of energy, and of life. It is the power center of your ego and of your identity, which transforms many times throughout your life. When you breathe with intention into this area of your body, you bring your true Self forth into the world. Can you bring your gifts forward? Inhale into the light of yourself and your worthiness, your spark of life. Exhale any congestion, confusion, energy of others, or undigested emotions. Keep breathing as you increase the presence of your beautiful, radiant light in your third chakra.

Then move your awareness to your chest. The fourth chakra is your heart chakra, the Anahata chakra. It is the air element fueled by your breath and circulation throughout your whole body and your energy system. It is typically green, sometimes with gold or pink in it. It is the power center of spiritual love, love for humanity, and self-love. The powers of the heart chakra are kindness, gratitude, generosity, oneness, compassion, and love. Exhale your potent and cleansing breath as you give grief space to be felt and dislodged. Breathe in and allow your heart to fill with light.

Now shift your awareness to your throat chakra. Your fifth chakra is the Vishuddha chakra. It is typically a blue power center, and its element is ether. This chakra is the power of your expression. It is the power of speaking truth and the power of intuitive listening. It's the power of expressing your higher Self and your lower self, or your human and emotional experience. It is about speaking universal truths and personal truths. It's the power of discernment, knowing when to talk and when to listen. Breathe light and purification into this center; exhale out suppression of your voice, held-back words, and held-back emotions. As you release, breathe light into this area of your throat and allow the light to purify the chakra for all space, time, and dimensions.

Then bring your awareness to your brow. The sixth chakra is your Ajna chakra, or your third eye center. Typically purple or indigo, it is the power of perception, visualization, higher knowing, realm of possibility, and intuition. It is the element of light and allows you to tune in to that which is bigger and more vast than the rational mind. Breathe light into this area of your body as you feel your legs and feet. Stay connected to your lower body while you allow light to cleanse doubt and clear away others' expectations of you. As you detox your third eye, allow light to illuminate this area and awaken the higher vision of you in your infinite potential.

Move your awareness now to the crown of your head. About six inches above the top of your head is a beautiful multicolored crown chakra that opens like a funnel to the Divine. This is the seventh chakra, known as the Sahasrara chakra. Its element is space. It is the gateway to faith in a higher power, some names of which may be God, grace, the Divine, the universe, the creator, infinite love, universal love. Whatever term you use, allow the divine light to pour in through your open seventh chakra. Allow it to release your mind and your ego. Release the contraction of your body; let go of working so hard on a mental and human level. Open up to receiving divine support and love through this spiritual connection. Open yourself to the realm of miracles and faith. Release doctrines that are not yours and that contradict your Soul's truth about what the Divine really is. You get to have your own subjective experience of the Divine. The crown chakra unlocks the relationship between your heart and the divine realm. It is the gateway to your prayer channel, allowing you to speak to and be heard by the universe.

Above your crown chakra is a beautiful golden sun. In that sun is infinite potential, healing light, and any intentions you would like to see fulfilled for yourself. Fill this golden sun with intentions for your Soul or your physical, mental, and emotional healing. Let those intentions swim inside the sun and build up vibrancy. Then turn this golden sun to liquid and allow it to pour through your open seventh chakra. Let it flow down through the crown of your head, your face, the back of your head, your neck, shoulders, chest, spine, all your central organs, your pelvis, your hips, and down through your legs and the soles of your feet. Let this light pulsate and radiate throughout your whole body. Let it extend beyond your physical body into the field of light around you and brighten the energy protecting the outside of your body.

Take some deep breaths here and allow yourself to glow. Embody your radiance until you feel complete.

JOURNALING EXERCISE

Following the meditation, take a moment to reflect on and journal about your experience of connecting to the power centers of your energy body.

1. Which aspects of your intuition (seeing, hearing, feeling, knowing) did you connect with in the guided meditation?
2. Did any inspirations, experiences, images, or impressions come to you?
3. As you moved through the meditation, did you have a sense of energy flowing through your chakras?

4. Were there places in your body where you felt your energy was blocked or stagnant?
5. Was there a chakra or area of your body that felt particularly weak or vacant?
6. Was there a chakra or area of your body that felt particularly strong?

It is helpful to reflect on the aspects of your intuition and your chakra system as you continue to work with the teachings and meditations in this book. From time to time you may want to return to your journal entries from earlier in your journey, to track changes in your experience and shifts in your awareness.

CHAPTER THREE

The Root Chakra and Your Family of Origin

As a Soul, you are light. You go in and out of lifetimes, and in each lifetime you create and absolve karma. You overcome something. You grow and evolve. From a state of expanded consciousness, you were born into the human experience to do this.

The root, or first, chakra is located in the tailbone area of your body. It is the power center that holds the consciousness of our safety, survival, and attachment to our material existence. The root chakra is the doorway to your ability to ground your energy into the earth and represents the earth element in your body. It governs your physical health; physical structures, such as your bones; your central nervous system; and your home life, which includes both your physical home and a sense of belonging or attachment to this world. It also governs innate love, often experienced as fullness and abundance, and attachment to your family of origin or chosen family.

This is the power center that houses deeply subconscious programming and information about your patterns, belief systems, and how you are going to operate in this world. Much of the energy held in the root chakra is part of your hard wiring, formed from the time you're in utero until the age of seven.

For empaths, it is crucial to understand the consciousness that's held at the root chakra. It is the foundation for your entire energy system, the patterns you repeat, and what you are holding on a subconscious level. That consciousness affects your ability to be connected to yourself deeply and to have strong, clear boundaries.

We are going to take a journey into the root chakra consciousness to unpack what is held in this region of the body.

Before birth, we incarnate in the womb. Because we are sentient beings who feel energy and operate through feeling, our empathic intuition is the first sense that forms. In the womb, our bodily systems and senses begin developing after the empathic sense is already established. We are not able to see, but we can hear somewhat as the ears form. While we're in the womb, the instinctual and sentient aspect of life is the primary state of being. With that comes a sensing of emotions as vibrations from our mother, father, family, and their history of beliefs and feelings.

Love and feeling wanted at deep levels are a primary form of bonding for an empathic or sensitive child, even while still in utero. Despite whatever emotions the mother experiences during pregnancy, the deeper bond of love for her child creates an attachment. After being born the empathic intuitive can feel what they have absorbed in the womb. If being unwanted is the deeper feeling here, this energy also forms part of a child's attachment in the world.

When we are born, we meet our family of origin or our adoptive family. We're awake in the world. In that experience, the empathic intuitive or sensitive child feels what is going on around them in a newfound, expanded space: being held, loved, fed, cleaned, and so on. Survival programming forms from how well we are attached to our family and feel the bonding. This attachment includes how we receive love, how safe we feel, whether there is peace, et cetera.

As we grow from infant to toddler to adolescent, we orient ourselves in our environment. We become attuned to our familial and cultural beliefs, whether they are spoken or enacted. If I am a sensitive child, I take that information in and bond to my family accordingly. As I internalize these beliefs, they become the beliefs I hold about myself. This is the foundation from which I will begin developing my belief systems.

In this environment, very sensitive beings can feel so much. The consciousness during a particular era influences familial and cultural beliefs. For example, fifty years ago, virtually no one was talking about how to nurture an intuitive child. Instead, parents were typically operating from beliefs and attitudes rooted in survival, social norms, and order, such as:

- *Children are to be seen, not heard.*
- *We keep quiet in this house.*
- *Don't make noise.*
- *It's not okay to have feelings.*
- *Don't trust anyone.*

These beliefs become part of the energy we marinate in as sensitive beings outside the womb. People in the household having beliefs and feelings is not unusual. What affects the sensitive child, though, is when an adult does not provide repair from trauma or upset, permission to be, or the sense of safety that comes from the child understanding that their feelings are warranted and true.

The child begins to lose a sense of belonging with the world — not always in the family, but in themselves. The energetic imprint is that the child, to survive, closes down to themselves in order to feel everyone else's energy around them. The loss of connection to self and to a sense of belonging is deeply subconscious in the root chakra. It innately forms the beginning of the overly empathic experience that we will be unpacking in this book.

To be an empowered empath, you must reclaim the power that exists in your root chakra. No longer are you a victim to the universe and to energy around you. The protection mechanisms you developed in childhood kept you safe and were appropriate for the time in life when you were vulnerable. Thank those protection mechanisms! Thank the disassociation, thank the fight-or-flight response, thank the pattern of overeating or whatever other repetitive pattern you adopted. These coping mechanisms were helping you during a time when you lacked power and love in your root chakra. As a spiritually progressing Soul in a human body who is on this earth to continuously grow and evolve, you are safe now, and it's absolutely okay for you to take back your power on behalf of your inner child.

Healing Inherited Belief Systems

Belief systems form deep in the energy body — imprinted in our spiritual DNA and connected to our human experiences. Positive belief systems form when we have bonding experiences in early childhood that make us feel safe and loved at a profound level. Positive bonding experiences can also help us recover from trauma. If a child experiences some form of repair that allows them to recover and regain a sense of safety, the experience will be less likely to become embedded in the energy body or evolve into complex trauma. However, when no repair or recovery occurs or the child is not protected or kept safe, the root chakra becomes imprinted with the experience, and fear-based belief systems may form as a result.

Fear-based beliefs are also referred to as negative belief systems. Some examples:

- *I'm not good enough.*
- *I'm unlovable.*
- *I'm not important.*
- *I'm not safe.*
- *I can't trust anyone.*
- *I'm inadequate.*
- *I'm a failure.*

These belief systems can be inherited from our family of origin, society, and/or culture. They are also born out of experiences that harm our sense of safety, validation, trust, or worthiness. Once we begin to understand the origins of our belief systems and how they come to form in our body, we start to uncover the history of our emotional and energetic patterns. This path of inquiry leads to a deeper exploration of trauma and its influence on our lives — and on our empathic intuition.

For now, I want to pause and give you a moment to journal about insights that have come from this chapter. Getting these insights out of your head and down on paper is part of processing them. Then take time to experience the guided meditation on the next page. This will support you with a felt sense of your inner child.

JOURNALING EXERCISE

This book is a journey into finding your power as an empath by understanding the subconscious patterns held in your energy field that contribute to your feeling disempowered. Below are some questions to support you in getting clear on who you are in your essence. Once you have read the questions, close your eyes, lean into your back body, and receive from your higher Self. Tune in and see what answers come from your intuition, then write them down.

1. What were the qualities of your true essence as a child? Were you a natural-born leader, creative, playful, full of joy, or something else? Describe the essence of you.
2. Did you feel seen, heard, and valued as a child?
3. What are the aspects of intuition that resonate for you most? For example, do you see intuitively, feel, hear, or know?
4. When did you learn that you were intuitive?
5. When did you learn you were an empath?
6. Do you feel seen, heard, and valued today?

• •

Guided Meditation:
Connecting to Your Inner Child's Essence
Audio version available at WendyDeRosa.com/book-meditations

• •

If listening to this meditation, close your eyes and go inward. If reading the meditation, pause and tune in to your higher Self after each section.

Take some deep breaths. Bring your attention to your root

chakra area and imagine the glowing essence of your inner child.

Amid all that was going on in the world around you when you were small, including everything everybody else was thinking and feeling, imagine picking up and holding your inner child in your lap.

Breathe and feel the essence of your inner child.

What does your inner child look like or feel like to you? What quality of energy does your inner child emanate?

Look your inner child in the eye. Tell your inner child, "For all the times that you did not feel held, seen, or connected with, I am here now. I see you. I hear you. I am holding you. I love you. You are worthy."

Take a moment and revel in your bond with your inner child right now. Feel it deep in your body, at the base of your spine. You are connecting to the part of you who has operated from feeling a little bit lost in the lower area of the body. Bring love to your inner child at this moment.

Take some deep breaths here and stay with this connection as long as you need to, giving attention to and holding your inner child.

CHAPTER FOUR

My Journey
as an Empathic Intuitive

Before we go further, I want to give you a window into my experience as an empath.

I was born into a family of eight kids in an Italian American household in Bridgeport, Connecticut. I was the oldest girl and the second oldest child. We were Roman Catholic, and I went to a multicultural Catholic school the majority of my school years, except for my last two years of high school. As you can imagine, one can't find a lot of space in a large family. Often there was a lot of projecting of emotions, and energy wasn't necessarily contained. Yet we were close as a family.

Back then I didn't know I was sensitive, and I certainly didn't know I had intuitive gifts. Instead, here is how it played out for me. Being the eldest daughter in a very large family, I took on the responsibility of caring for my younger siblings. That became my identity, something my energy body automatically did without question. I have more memories of observing my siblings having fun than of me participating in the fun. Being a child wasn't for me; it was for everyone except me. I was managing so much responsibility and pressure that I internalized it and pushed myself even harder. I felt overly responsible, deeply insecure, and unloved, despite being told I was loved. I was isolated. I immersed myself in music. I would sit at the piano, write songs, and put myself into another world so I could dream about what might be possible for me. Reflecting back, I suppose those dreams were fueled by a voice inside that had a bigger mission for me in this life.

I started to gain weight around age six. By the time I was ten, I had significant weight on me. Looking back, I'm sure I had undiagnosed food sensitivities, and emotional weight was accumulating. I didn't have anyone naming that or helping me through it because it wasn't common in the 1970s to look at food sensitivities and psychological or energetic imprinting. Instead, I was just the fat kid.

Times were tough back then. My father lost work because of the recession. Money issues increased. We would go days without heat, water, a phone, electricity. We eventually lost our home. Being one of the older kids, I felt the stress of my parents trying to manage life. I felt like the shabby kid trying to break away from a deep pain of humiliation. And I believed in more for myself.

I got sick a lot, particularly with strep throat, which I know now is related to the throat chakra and to the suppression of my true feelings. By the age of twelve I was developing noticeable signs of anxiety. I was also nannying for twenty-one families in my neighborhood to help pay the bills at home. I was often the first babysitter called because I was respected for being so responsible. By the time I was fourteen, I was subcontracting babysitting jobs out to my younger sister. I knew how to work hard, and I knew how to take care of people.

My anxiety and insecurities increased as my sensitivities increased. Crowds, loud noises, and being social were triggers for panic attacks. I would retreat into isolation to manage my anxiety and oversensitivity. When I was nineteen, I had a nervous breakdown. Little did I know that this breakdown was actually a door opening.

The nervous breakdown happened my sophomore year of college in Boston. At the time, I was feeling a strong call to move to Colorado. I knew nothing about Colorado except what I saw in a magazine. Colorado represented space, expansion, freedom, and, eventually, my next home.

A miracle happened while I was recovering from that nervous breakdown, trying to decide if I should leave school and move to Boulder to start a new life or stay and finish my studies.

One night, my college roommate and I decided to go for a walk down Newbury Street. Despite it being a chilly night, it felt good to walk after all I'd been through. The question I was trying to work out in my mind was: Should I finish out the semester at school, or should I leave right away, in my post-panic-attack state? Having just gone through an emotional breakdown, it was a stressful decision for me to have to make; I couldn't find my way clear to making a rational choice.

As I puzzled over my situation, struggling to find an answer that would bring me peace, my friend and I were approached by a man carrying a ukulele. He asked whether he could sing us a song in return for spare change. We brushed him off, saying, "No, but thanks anyway." Then the man looked at me and kindly stated, "I think you need to hear a song. Don't worry about the change."

He was dressed simply, wearing a red jacket. He had sandy-colored hair, and his head glowed as if surrounded by a halo. All at once, the whole world around me faded away; the street disappeared, and all I could see was this person with an angelic glow around his head. I was mesmerized by his presence. He told us his name was Arias, and then he began his song: "Home on the range where the buffalo roam…one day you'll get to Colorado…" I was in shock; it was as if he knew what my struggle was. Then he said to me: "Wendy" — I hadn't told him my name — "it's not time to go yet. You will get there. Just hang in there a little longer." Then he kissed me on the cheek and ran off. My roommate and I looked at each other in disbelief, and then we looked around to see where he had gone, but he was nowhere to be seen. We walked up and down the street and checked in the shops, but Arias had completely vanished.

I knew he was an angel. My roommate knew he was an angel. There was no doubt in our minds, and we were filled with joy. I called my mom, a devout Catholic, and she said, "Wendy, I prayed to the angel Arias because I knew he could reach you through song."

A miracle had occurred that night for me. Following my encounter with Arias, the anxiety and emotional struggle I'd been experiencing went away. I had received a healing and felt watched over. I set my goal to finish out the semester, and I completed it with inspiration from divine support.

The following summer I moved to Colorado, where my intuitive development and energy healing journey began. I found a teacher to study with in Boulder, and my gift opened up as I continued to experience spiritual awakening. In my twenties I was focused on launching my career as a musician, but I began offering intuitive healing sessions on the side. I had transferred into a new college and changed my major to humanities with an emphasis in music; I was also practicing playing guitar seven hours a day. After college, I was in a band and toured as a singer-songwriter. I tried to make it but struggled, pushing from a very wounded ego and ultimately hurting myself and others along the way. It became increasingly difficult to reconcile the awakenings I was experiencing with the other areas of my life. I felt more and more disconnected from my desire to be a musician.

Although my anxiety had subsided, I still felt wounded. I was hurting, and I was acting out. I wanted to sing and be heard. I wanted to be seen and valued. Inside I was filled with pain and aching from trauma and from my inner child's need for deep love and reparenting. I didn't feel loved — and worse, I felt unlovable. My mind told me that of course I was loved, but my heart couldn't feel it.

Filled with the resolve that the answer was to try harder, push through, overcome, I moved to the San Francisco Bay Area to finally become a professional musician. It was no longer my love for music that motivated me. I was no longer inspired. I was completely being run by my unconscious wounded ego.

I was pushy.

I was "too sensitive."

I needed attention.

I was absorbing energy around me.

I gained weight again.

I projected my emotions onto others.

I absorbed the pain of others.

I felt screamed at by the world and scolded myself internally.

Nothing seemed good enough because I didn't feel like I was good enough.

Shame, guilt, anger, grief, and fear were my unwelcome teachers. Yet I wasn't taking responsibility for those feelings at the time. Instead, I was competitive and jealous toward others in music, trying to push my way onto stages to be seen as a musician. I was walking wounded, and I tried to medicate my hurt by letting my ego drive my music. I was still committed to my meditations and to listening to my angels' and guides' communications. It was actually humbling. On the one hand, I was self-destructing from unprocessed childhood pain, and on the other hand, I was being called from within to understand more about my gift of intuition, because it was getting stronger and I could see that people I offered sessions to were healing.

In my late twenties, my spiritual guides were at my back, nudging me with intense love to say yes to my gift. My practice grew to the point where I realized I needed to take my work as an intuitive healer seriously. Friends were encouraging me. Literally, I looked up to the sky one day and said, "Okay, I'll do it. I'll be an intuitive healer."

By the time I was thirty, I had more than five hundred clients from all over the world, and just from word of mouth — social media didn't exist back then! Profound downloads would come through me for my clients. From these powerful sessions, people were experiencing deep healing — finding relief from chronic health issues, emotional trauma, and energetic blockages. I was humbled and honored to bear witness to their transformation.

I also continued my own path of healing. Previously, even though I had been taking all the right steps to become healthy, I would slip into an old pattern of being overly sensitive and disempowered, leading to emotional struggle and energetic overwhelm. This finally changed for me when I said yes to my healing gift. I was not only saying yes to my calling, I was finally shifting into alignment with my divine Self and inhabiting my body and my power fully.

Eventually I started to teach intuitive healing. Through years of case studies, looking at thousands of people's energetic systems, listening to my higher guidance (through meditation, deep yoga study, writing books, and listening inwardly), public teaching, self-healing, falling down and picking myself back up again, and yet more deep intuitive listening, I have gained a profound understanding of how intuition is innate within each of us, how it relates to the chakra system, and how embracing it makes us whole. What I know now that I did not know back then is that I am clairvoyant, clairaudient, clairsentient, and claircognizant — that I was intuitively seeing, hearing, feeling, and knowing.

When I began my healing journey, I was consumed by my wounds. I had been born into an environment where I was conditioned to lose my sense of self, abandon my center, and exist without any energetic or emotional boundaries. Once I accepted that I had a gift, I began to realize my childhood experiences did not define me. I learned that I was actually intuitive and could help people. I started to feel connected to my innate healing ability and embody my power. I still experience life's ups and downs, but I have greater access to my Self, I inhabit my physical and energetic body more fully, and

I connect to Source and my guidance anytime I need support. Today, I love myself and feel resourced with tools to navigate this dynamic world.

Although your story may be different from mine, I believe you were born with a gift, too. I believe you may have had life experiences that clouded your intuitive abilities and may carry inherited patterns that have kept you from embodying your gifts. I believe your sensitivity to energy is actually a signal, guiding you back to your intuition. I believe your physical, emotional, or mental symptoms hold wisdom and guidance for you, just like mine did for me. I also believe that your Soul chose to incarnate at this time and that you embodying your true light is exactly what this planet needs for collective healing.

JOURNALING EXERCISE

Take some time to journal on your personal story, looking at it through the lens of what you have just learned about patterns you may have imprinted in your lower body, especially in your first and second chakras.

1. What was your story as it relates to your awareness of being overly sensitive, intuitive, and empathic?
2. Was there a pivotal moment in your life when you believe an angel was present or the Divine had your back?
3. What are your gifts? What is so innately you that you overlook it as a gift?
4. Have you said yes to your gifts? If not, what is in the way of you accepting your gifts?

Guided Meditation:
Connecting with Your Inner Guidance
Audio version available at WendyDeRosa.com/book-meditations

Close your eyes and take some deep breaths. As you breathe, let your body settle, allow your muscles to relax, and slow down your inner tempo.

Tune in to answer the questions: Was there a time in my life when I was being guided? Was I being guided by my own inner light? Was I being guided by something bigger than me, such as angels or the divine universe?

Take a moment, breathe, and allow the insights to come.

Now, bring your awareness to your heart center and feel, or imagine, the glowing light of your Soul radiating with truth and knowing.

Inner guidance can be felt in many places in the body: in your heart, in your gut, and even in your mind. All are potent power centers for intuition. Relax the frontal lobe of your brain, connect to the light of your Soul, and listen. Feel your Soul's wisdom come through.

You can recite these words: "I am slowing down to listen inward and to trust you more. I am willing to believe in miracles. I trust the miraculous. Thank you for guiding me. I am sorry I override you with fear and worry. I will relax, surrender, and listen. I trust my inner guidance."

Breathe deeply as you make room for your inner guidance to take up space in your consciousness and in your body. Let it resolve the anxiety, stress, or worry with trust.

Take several more deep breaths here, and take as much time as you need to feel the power of your inner guidance.

CHAPTER FIVE

Grounding Your Energetic Anatomy

We all know how revitalizing it is to be in nature: connecting with the natural world, stimulating your senses, and filling your lungs with oxygen lifts your mood and spirit. Grounding is simply the process of connecting your body with the earth. You can do this effortlessly by walking barefoot on the earth, digging your toes into the sand, or resting your body on soft grass and rich soil.

Grounding is critical for intuitives and empaths and is an essential aspect of one's daily practice. Especially when energy is scattered or out of balance, it is important to direct the energy flowing in and around your body into the earth. You can also draw up the earth's energy to help you ground your entire energy body.

The earth's surface carries biocurrents that defuse the electric charges that build up in the physical body. If allowed to accumulate, these charges can affect the nervous system, your health, and your wellbeing, leaving you feeling ungrounded.

Historically, human beings have been more connected to the earth than we are today. Western civilization has paved over and built upon much of the earth's surface. As a result, our connection to this vital life-force energy has greatly diminished, affecting our physical and mental health. However, there are many effective ways to restore our grounding. From the perspective of our energetic anatomy, we ground through an energetic root system that extends from our hips, our sitz bones, and our feet into the earth. Like the meridians in Traditional Chinese Medicine, these are not anatomical systems; rather, they are energetic systems that channel energy throughout the body, through the energy field around the physical body, and into the earth. We call this energetic root a *grounding cord*, which is an energetic line that connects our root chakra to the vibration of the center of the earth. This grounding cord supplies vital life-force energy to our physical body to nourish our organs, calm our nervous system, and support our energetic anatomy. When this line of energy is intact, it instills in us a feeling of safety and trust and a strong sense of self. When we are ungrounded or the grounding cord is not fully intact, we can feel scattered, confused, overly emotional, anxious, unsafe; we experience racing thoughts, irrational fears, codependency, insecurity, and the loss of a sense of self.

I like to think of the grounding cord as a wide pillar that is secured around the hips, the low belly, and the low spine. This pillar extends deep into the earth's core and grounding vibration. Sometimes the grounding cord is perceived as a skinny cord from the tailbone to the center of the earth, but I like to widen the image in order to provide a greater sense of stability and a secure attachment to the base of our bodies. Other times the grounding cord is compared to a tree trunk, an image that evokes a connection with the earth element and an extensive root system. Similar to the root chakra, the grounding cord also carries the bond to our familial and cultural history that subconsciously informs how we are going to operate in the world.

The grounding cord is a channel of energy that connects your body to the center of the earth. An empath's grounding cord provides them with an incredible sense of calm and clarity.

It's especially important for empaths to replenish or fuel the base of our body with vital earth energy through our grounding cord. If not enough earth energy is supporting the base of the body, energy from the lower body is pushed upward. When this happens, our upper chakras expand and open to support the amount of energy that is moving through them. We lose the balance between the upper and lower body, essentially becoming more high functioning in the upper chakras and more closed down in the lower chakras.

If we have not developed grounding tools or techniques to reconnect to nature and settle our nervous system, it's possible to live chronically ungrounded. This means that over many years, the body has acquired a pattern that makes it feel safer for you to live high up in your head or your heart and to be disconnected from the power in your lower body. On an energetic level, we start to accumulate wounds and unprocessed energy in the lower chakras. When we do try to ground, it can cause fatigue; it can feel emotional or fearful. Grounding isn't always comfortable, especially if we have been trained to mirror an ungrounded society that emphasizes rational processing instead of truth, peace, calm, and connection.

Why Grounding Is Important to Support Healthy Intuition

Our thoughts are influenced by the life experiences and imprints that we store in our energy body. If our thoughts relate to an experience that felt fearful or threatening, our body is going to react in a way to protect us from experiencing fear or threat again. These responses become wired into our thinking and our unconscious beliefs.

Intuition is divine consciousness communicating through our body. Whether we experience our intuition as an inner voice, a higher Self, a sense of knowing, or a kinesthetic response in the body, it is clearest when we are grounded, calm, and connected to the present moment. When we are in a triggered state, we are not grounded in the present moment. Our thoughts are racing, taking us back to the time and place of the initial wounding. In this temporary regressed state, we are cut off from our intuition, inner knowing, and higher guidance.

People often ask, "Is this my fear talking, or is it my intuition?" In some cases it could be both. If the fear is meant to keep us out of danger, it is our intuition. However, when the "monkey mind" — the unsettled, restless mind — is racing, your thoughts can create more anxiety. You become disconnected from yourself and must ground your body before you can access clear guidance. When the mind settles, a new current of consciousness awakens in the body — your intuition!

These days, with all that is happening on the planet, you might wonder, "Should I really be grounding into the earth when there is such chaos right now?" Some spiritual teachers advise against it in such times. From my experience, however, birth, death, and rebirth are elements in the cycle of life. We are part of a rising consciousness that is evolving through a process of destruction, the evolution of consciousness, and subsequent re-creation. As structures dismantle, new ways are revealed. In times of collective trauma, such as a pandemic, racial injustice, or natural disaster, the most important thing you can do is to notice what issues arise for you, process them, and then deepen your grounding. We incarnated at this time to be part of what is unfolding, and we need to stay grounded in order to live from our deeper truth and fulfill our rightful purpose. As consciously evolving beings, it is critical that we not give in to spiritual bypassing, transcending what is happening rather than experiencing it fully. We are here to be part of the solution through our own inner work.

So, to go back to the question about whether we should ground while the world is in this state, the short answer is: yes — and ground ever more deeply.

JOURNALING EXERCISE

Draw a picture of your grounding cord. In your journal, reflect on these questions:

1. What does it look like?
2. Do the roots grow deep into the earth or stay close to the surface?
3. What color is your grounding cord?
4. What does grounding mean to you?
5. What are some ways that you like to ground?

Guided Meditation: Your Grounding Cord
Audio version available at WendyDeRosa.com/book-meditations

Take a comfortable seat. Close your eyes and bring your attention to your sitz bones and pelvic bowl.

Imagine a tree trunk secure around the sides of your hips, your low belly, and your low spine. See it extend down deep through the layers of the earth.

In the center of the earth, the tree sprouts roots around the core of the planet. Feel the sense of security, safety, and trust this provides to your energetic system.

Breathe and imagine that at the base of this tree, which is your grounding cord, you discover the den of a beautiful earth mother. She invites you to sit and rest on a comfortable sofa in her den, and she offers you a cup of tea meant to soothe you and release any energy within you that is ready to be let go.

In her compassion, she asks you to give to her anything that does not serve you. She will transmute any negative energy in the center of the earth.

Take some deep breaths. As you drink in the tea, allow your body to let go of any subconscious fears you carry that have been deeply resting within yourself.

Breathe. Let yourself ground profoundly into your body. Grounding is slow, so it may take some time to feel settled. Continue to breathe and ground into your being until you feel nurtured and complete.

CHAPTER SIX

Your Energetic System from the Empathic Perspective

Let's take a deeper look at the body's energetic system and how your first three chakras are closely tied to your empathic intuition.

As we've been exploring, the chakras hold an immense amount of information. The lower chakras relate to our humanity and how we attach and bond to one another in the physical realm; they are also where our spirit bonds with our physical body. The lower power centers hold our personal needs for safety, trust, emotions, identity, and the creative expression of who we are in the world. They also carry processed and unprocessed wounds, called *imprints*, that may become hardwired into our nervous system, our habits, and how we think and relate in the world. Imprints encompass all types of information that is stored in the body through someone's experience. Negative imprints that are inherited through DNA and through our culture and/or passed down through family behavior are called *inherited wounds*.

Like genetic material that is encoded in your body's DNA, your chakras are encoded with information about your spiritual DNA — experiences in this lifetime, imprints from your lineage, and your Soul's entire history. Your lower chakras also carry inherited wounds, such as grief, pain, and feelings of powerlessness, which cause energy-body imbalances that become embedded in those chakras.

In addition, the lower power centers make up part of the ego. The word *ego* has a negative connotation; however, we really need a healthy ego to function in the world. I like to think of the ego as having two possible expressions: a healthy one and a wounded one.

A healthy ego is the part of us that contains our God-given gifts. It is the vehicle through which we manifest our true Self in the world. We must nurture this healthy part, because through it we express our divine essence.

We also have a wounded ego. This part contains fear, which gives rise to negative thoughts and limiting beliefs. It also holds trauma, which informs our conditioning and reactions to the world. The wounded ego interrupts the voice of our true Soul, which is our intuition and inner guidance.

Our life's path is to dismantle the wounded ego in order to live from truth, so that we can exist in the world with meaning, purpose, and harmony. We create and pass on a lot of damage when we operate from a wounded ego. We project our worries onto others, looking for them to nurture and "fix" us, and we can't feel the light of our true Self. We are all called upon to do the work necessary to heal our damaged ego and radiate clear light. As empaths heal the inherited wounds and imprints in their lower three chakras, the healthy ego can emerge.

When imbalances become embedded in the lower chakras,

feeling wounded rather than empowered can seem normal to an empath. It takes time and expanded awareness for empowered energy to begin to feel good and become the new normal for an empath.

As I've mentioned, the first chakra, or the root chakra, is the power center for stability and trust in yourself. It controls the flow of energy between the tailbone of your body and the center of the earth. When we become frightened, our root chakra contracts, stopping the flow of our energy to the center of the earth, and we become cut off from a vital sense of grounding. If we experienced early childhood trauma or felt unsafe or that we didn't belong, then the root chakra has likely remained contracted, creating an underlying sense of feeling unstable. Some people live their whole lives with a blocked or contracted root chakra, relying on coping mechanisms to help them survive. (In chapter 8, I discuss in detail the impact of a contracted root chakra and how it leads to hypervigilance and an inability to maintain boundaries.)

The second chakra is where we carry our emotional self, and the third chakra is where we hold our boundaries and power in relation to the world around us. A contraction in the first chakra will cause the second and third chakras to become imbalanced, making the empath lose their sense of self and disconnect from their lower chakras. Not only does this leave them vulnerable to other people's energy, they will actively draw in other people's energy to fill this void.

Clearly, the lower three chakras play a significant role in an empath's ability to stop taking on the energy of others. It is critical for empaths to reclaim these power centers.

When the first three chakras are functioning in a healthy manner, they create a solid foundation for the rest of the chakras. However, when the lower chakras are imbalanced, the upper chakras are impacted as well.

While our Soul exists throughout our body, our primary connection to it is through our upper chakras. We become walled off from this and other spiritual connections through the life experiences and cultural conditioning that contributed to the imbalances in the lower chakras. As we evolve through our personal journeys, these barriers dissolve, and the upper chakras can open up. We are able to reconnect with our Soul and access deeper levels of consciousness.

Some people come into this world with very open upper chakras. They are already awake and have heightened intuition in the upper power centers. In this case, their work is to ground themselves in their lower body and chakras and embody their upper-chakra power in the physical realm. They can do this by expressing the gifts of the upper chakras, such as leadership directed by their higher guidance. Such leaders are often luminaries, teachers, authors, and speakers who help contribute to the awakening of others.

Just as the lower chakras are connected to empathic intuition, the upper chakras are linked to psychic intuition. (In my work I don't often use the word *psychic*, because it refers only to the upper half of the intuitive body.) The upper-body intuition and lower-body intuition converge in the heart chakra. It is through the heart chakra, as well as our lower chakras, that we are connected to our claircognizant sense. This includes the deep heart callings, the inner knowing, and the union between the spiritual experience and the human experience. The phrase "listen to your heart" means "listen to your Soul in union with the Divine." This is how you connect to the part of you that navigates your life's mission. The heart chakra unifies the higher knowing and psychic realms with the lower-body intuition, emotions, attachments, and experiences of the human condition.

The heart chakra is a major center for intuition and empathy. Whether we feel clear in the heart depends on what we are energetically holding in the lower body's first three chakras.

Upper-Body Intuitives and Lower-Body Intuitives

Intuition, as I've said, is the emergence of the Soul's light and consciousness through the power centers of the body. For some people, more of their emerging power and light will come through their lower power centers. I call these people *lower-body intuitives*. For others, who are *upper-body intuitives*, more will come through their upper chakras. And for many it will be a blend of both.

Lower-body intuitives tend to get gut feelings or feel energy that is not spoken. They have empathy and the ability to relate to others, and people typically share vulnerably with lower-body intuitives. Yet they often merge energetically with others in conversations and take on their energy. They are also prone to becoming overwhelmed by emotions.

Upper-body intuitives easily connect to the Divine and hear their higher Self, spirit guides, and angels. They see images in their minds as well as energy attached to other people or present in the world around them. They tend to have a higher vision and perceive the big picture, with an expanded awareness of the planet. Messages often come through to them when they write. They can find it hard to quiet their minds.

Not all upper-body intuitives are grounded into their lower body, and not all lower-body intuitives are open to the divine flow in their upper body. Likewise, not all empaths identify as being psychic, and not all psychics relate to being empaths. It is the path of the holistic intuitive to learn how to embody and express all aspects of the chakra system in order to have healthy, grounded, and centered intuition.

In the energetic system, the true Self shows up as consciousness that emerges in the central channel of our body, the powerful pipeline of life-force energy that runs from the crown of our head down to our tailbone. The consciousness that travels through that central channel is divine energy in communion with our Soul's light.

Ideally, nothing would be in that central channel but our Self and God. However, we are human beings, and lots of things get into the central channel. You know that an energetic experience has impacted your central channel when you carry a wound that has rocked you to the core. These are called core wounds, and they take time to heal. They are surrounded by many layers of conditioning, coping mechanisms, and protection, and they contain many aspects to be resolved. The central channel runs through the center of the chakras, and depending on where the wound has landed, it will manifest in the chakra related to that area. I will discuss the central channel in greater detail in chapter 7.

JOURNALING EXERCISE

After reading this chapter, take some time to consider how you relate to the different types of intuition described. Use your journal to respond to these questions:

1. Do you resonate with being more of an upper-body intuitive or a lower-body intuitive? Or both?

2. Do you resonate with being clairvoyant, clairaudient, clairsentient, or claircognizant? Or with any combination or all four aspects of intuition?

3. In what ways do you experience seeing intuitively, hearing intuitively, feeling intuitively, and knowing intuitively? For example, do you see images? Do you hear higher guidance? Do you feel energy around you? Does your body show you physical symptoms to get your attention?

Guided Meditation: Grounding Upper-Body Intuition and Uplifting Lower-Body Intuition
Audio version available at WendyDeRosa.com/book-meditations

Take a comfortable seat and close your eyes. From your sitz bones, allow your grounding cord to extend down deep into the earth and sprout roots.

Breathe deeply.

Now imagine bringing your grounding cord up a little higher around the sides of your hips, your low belly, and your lower spine.

Let your grounding cord secure the base of your body and see it as a strong pipeline or tree trunk to the center of the earth.

Breathe deeply and allow the connection to the earth to ground you.

Then call all your energy into your body from anywhere it has been wandering or from anyone your energy has been with.

Breathe.

Once you are settled in your body, tune in to the question "Am I a lower-body intuitive?" Do you get gut feelings or feel energy that is not spoken? Do you often merge energetically with others in conversations and take on their energy? Do you get overwhelmed by emotions? Do you feel the energy of others? If so, allow the top of your grounding cord to rise to your waistline and secure your lower chakras. Feel a sense of protection in the front of your belly and pelvis.

Breathe as you allow the lower half of your body to feel secure within the presence of your grounding cord.

Now, tune in and ask yourself: "Am I an upper-body intuitive?" Do you connect to the divine realm and hear spirit guides and angels? Do you see images in your mind? Do you see energy in others or in the world around you? Do you have a higher vision and see the big picture? Do you have an expanded awareness of the planet? Do messages come through when you write?

Excess life-force energy in the upper body can make the mind race and will unground you. If you find it hard to quiet your mind, take some deep breaths and allow any excess energy in your head or upper body to settle down and descend through your grounding cord into your seat, as if your Soul is taking a deep seat in your body. Your visions and heightened awareness in your upper chakras will become clearer as you ground yourself and listen to your lower body's intuition.

You are balancing the energy between your upper body and lower body. Breathe here.

If you are someone who is both an upper-body and a lower-body intuitive, continue breathing. Allow the security of your grounding cord to hold your lower body, and allow any excess energy in your upper body to relax, become calm, and settle.

Keep breathing here as you allow your upper body to balance with your lower body and vice versa. Take as much time as you need. Your body will come into balance if you create space for it to do so.

Let this meditation be a foundation for balancing your upper-body intuition and your lower-body intuition so that you can be integrated as the intuitive being that you are.

Breathe.

When you are ready, you can slowly open your eyes.

CHAPTER SEVEN

Your Central Channel, the Pillar of Light

As we discussed in chapter 5, grounding is the connection between our physical bodies and the earth's frequency. It allows us to access the center of our body, which in the energetic anatomy is referred to as the *central channel* or the *pillar of light*. This channel is a meridian that runs in front of the spine through the chakras. In yoga it is called the Sushumna nadi, and it sends life-force energy throughout the energetic system. As more life-force and divinity move through the central channel of the body, light radiates from the center of your being, forming a pillar of light.

The central channel contains the essence of your Soul in union with divine consciousness. Ideally, nothing would be in the central channel but the light of your Soul and the Divine, or the universe. Because we are human, core wounds exist within the central channel and include imprints, unconscious beliefs, and soul contracts (unconscious agreements we make with others in this lifetime and beyond to fulfill roles in one another's lives). Some core wounds are from past lives, your ancestral lineage, or karma from previous lifetimes. To clear these embedded wounds, bring your conscious awareness to them with the intention of healing and releasing them. You can then process them through emotional and therapeutic work, energy healing, movement, breath work, yoga, and many other modalities. If you find that you are not able to do this on your own, I recommend that you reach out to a practitioner, therapist, or healer for support.

The more significant a core wound is, the more embedded it will be. Even if you are doing the work to move the wound out, it can take a lifetime to migrate from the central channel to the periphery of your body. And even once it releases from the central channel, it may not be fully released from your consciousness, habits, or behaviors. Being aware that a core wound is deeply embedded and where it exists in the body will help you shift its energy. After you have created some separation from the wound and it no longer defines you, you can approach it more easily and with more objectivity.

Your light and divine essence can then expand and reclaim that space where the wound has been released. The grounding cord is essential to this process: it provides earth energy to the base of the body where it connects with the pillar of light. At the upper end of the pillar of light, the crown chakra opens to grace. This area at the top of the head is where we take in cosmic life-force energy, which fills the pillar of light from above. This infusion of earth energy from below and cosmic life-force from above illuminates the central channel of the body.

Your Front Body and Back Body

The central channel acts as an anchor for your spiritual stamina and inner radiance. Most of us live out of the front side of our chakras and energy body. We engage with the world through the front of our head, throat, heart, belly, and pelvis. Essentially, this is the ego consciousness of the energy system, the conditioning that we were raised in. It shapes our experiences and informs how we navigate and survive in the world. Through the front body we interact, organize our thoughts, form attachments with others, and process the world around us.

We also have a back side to our body and a back side to our chakras. The back side is where we bring power and nourishment to the Self. It's where we connect to the deeper aspects of our inner world and to the Divine. Shifting our awareness from our front body into our back body allows us to feel our center more powerfully. Back-body consciousness can be cultivated through acts of self-care, meditation, and prayer. Many of us go through our lives engaged only in the front side of the energy system, cut off from the back side and becoming depleted energetically, limiting our ability to be introspective and to listen to our intuition. Front-body consciousness by itself never leaves us with a feeling of being met fully or having our cup filled.

Think of your central channel as having a front and a back side, and imagine that you are infusing your body with a waterfall of light and receptivity from the Divine. It flows through the entire central pillar of your body. I like to encourage people to emphasize the light essence showering down through the back body, as though they are leaning back into overflowing grace. Of course it also showers the front body, but because we tend to be front-body focused, it is a shift to think about the back body in this way. It can be a game changer to allow grace to flow through the back side of your energy body!

When teaching this concept, I often tell teachers, care-givers, parents, healers, therapists, and others to focus on the back side of their heart. If you are in a caregiving position, frequently you are giving so much from the front of your heart that you need to bring your awareness to the back of your heart in order to be able to receive unconditional love. The grace of the Divine is meeting you in your tired, depleted, or emotional heart, so that you can be nourished, uplifted, and connected to love and higher consciousness.

Why Is the Central Channel Important for Empaths?

The pillar of light in an empath's body is their center. Empaths who live primarily in the front side of their energy system tend to get into codependent relationships. They have difficulty with boundaries and lose connection to themselves. They often operate unconsciously from wounded programming that stems from childhood.

As an empath, the practices you are learning here will help you cultivate a connection to your inner self and back-body consciousness. To truly heal, you can't just visualize the pillar of light; you must do the deeper work, unravel the energy, feel it, process it, and release it. The aim is to purify the central channel and your energy system through deep, conscious awareness of what you're holding in your energy body. The meditations you have been doing in this book are building the energetic foundation that will enable you to inhabit more of your central channel. As you uncover the wounds and negative programming held there, you will begin to understand how they have impacted your ability to stand in your power. Strengthening your back body and your central channel empowers you to live as an embodied empath.

True energetic boundaries come from directing the newfound energy in your central channel to your power centers, or chakras. You will begin to radiate the presence of your innate power and who you are as an intuitive being in this life. Strong energetic boundaries become the new normal. These new imprints in your energy body then become grounded into your physical body.

JOURNALING EXERCISE

Tune in and sense your central channel. Then consider these questions:

1. What does it feel like to you? Are there areas that are more vibrant than others?
2. What happens when you breathe light into areas of your central channel that have been carrying wounds?
3. Draw a picture of your central channel with light flowing down the front and back sides of your body. Do you have any newfound senses or awareness of your back body?

Guided Meditation:
The Front and Back Sides of the Pillar
Audio version available at WendyDeRosa.com/book-meditations

Take a comfortable seat. Begin by breathing deeply into your low belly.

Slow down your thoughts and take as much time as you

need to let your body settle. Feel your grounding cord secure around your hips, your sitz bones, your low belly, and your lower spine. Imagine it extending down deep into the center of the earth and sprouting roots.

Rising tall from your tailbone and pelvic floor is your radiant central channel. Take some deep breaths into this main meridian for divine light and the infinite light of your Soul.

Notice if you tend to be more open in the front of your body, receiving the world and engaging with the world.

Now imagine that you're leaning back into a beautiful waterfall of grace. That waterfall is cleansing your back body and opening consciousness there. Breathe and allow this light to cleanse and strengthen your spiritual backbone. Breathe. Let that waterfall of light then shower over the top of your head and cleanse your front body, washing off anything that doesn't serve you in the front of your aura. Breathe.

Now bring your awareness to the central channel of your body. In an ideal state, nothing should be in the central channel but the light of your true Soul and divine consciousness or love. However, you are human, and experiences and imprints have embedded themselves in your central channel throughout your Soul's lifetimes. Take some deep breaths and allow the shower of light to pour down through the crown of your head. Breathe that light through your central channel. On your exhales, let go of any energy blockages, stuck energy, emotions, density — anything that the power of your light-infused breath can clear from your system.

Any energy held in the central channel of the body is a core imprint, or a core wound, or a core belief system. It can be very subconscious, embedded in a blind spot and hardwired into how you operate. As you breathe deeply into your central channel, you're moving energy from your blind spot to the periphery of your energy body so you can see it and release it. Energy releases when we take responsibility for having it.

Use your grounding cord as a depository for any energy that doesn't serve you. Let it release the energy down into the earth, where the divine earth mother can dissolve it.

Breathe.

You are worthy of having your center. It's your divine right to embody the light of your Soul. Breathe here and allow the fresh, clean light moving through your central channel to radiate and increase the presence of your vibrancy. You are becoming embodied love in this moment.

Feel and allow love to radiate from the center of your being. This doesn't have to be love that you give away just yet. It's love between you and the Divine. It's love just for you. It's your innate essence owning this moment.

Breathe. Feel. Be present. Radiate.

All the love that you want and need from the world is here inside you, right now.

Breathe.

Feel the power of this love form a bubble of light all the way around you for protection and for integration of this meditation.

Take as much time as you need to marinate in the power and radiance of your central channel. Take a mental snapshot of this moment, and state an intention for your day or for your life.

When you are ready, slowly open your eyes and bring your embodied presence into the world.

CHAPTER EIGHT

The Effects of Root Chakra Contraction on Your Empathic Intuition

When your safety is compromised by a real or perceived threat, your root chakra contracts. It closes down at the base of the spine as a means of self-preservation. This reaction can be triggered when you feel unsafe at a fundamental level or when you feel that "it's not safe to be me." If you were raised in an unstable home or experienced childhood trauma, this response can also become a default setting.

The second and third chakras are emotional power centers that feel energy. When the root chakra contracts, your second and third chakras overcompensate either by blowing wide open or by shutting down. When this happens, you lose your sense of self and shift your focus to energy outside of yourself. This is where *hypervigilance*, a state of increased alertness, gets activated. Hypervigilance in the energetic body is a survival response. Your second and third chakras go into overdrive, and you scan others energetically for what they need so you can meet those needs in order to make yourself safe.

When this pattern becomes ingrained, it feels normal to disconnect from yourself in order to make sure everyone else's needs are being met. This is where an empathic intuitive's natural gift shifts from the ability to sense energy to being overly empathic. Hypervigilance becomes a way of life. Your root chakra energy doesn't flow or allow you to ground into your own body or into the earth. As a result, you are overly attentive to others at the expense of your own needs, health, and wellbeing.

When the root chakra contracts, our life-force energy becomes concentrated in the upper chakras and upper body, more diffuse in the lower chakras and lower body. Our energetic center then moves higher to protect itself from feeling the struggle or trauma held in the lower body. Under stress, the Soul's energy can move out of the body entirely, opening the door for other people's energy to come into that space. This is not the same as being impacted by other people's so-called negative energy. We absorb other people's energy (positive or negative) because we are not fully occupying our own energy body.

With our conscious awareness shifted higher in the body, we can still be high functioning in the upper chakras and even highly intuitive, connected to spirit guides, angels, and other dimensions. What will happen over time, however, is that we create a chronic vacancy in the lower body. You may become vulnerable, experiencing life at the effect of others, and prone to feeling like a victim, rather than living from your power. Wounds also fill the vacancy in the lower body. These wounds do not just go away; they grab our attention when we get triggered, or they create symptoms in our physical, emotional, or energetic body. Being triggered can actually be a positive experience if we take it as an opportunity to see where we are not grounded or not holding our power. Chronic conditions can also be an opportunity for transformation. We can embrace the experience holistically and recognize that these imbalances are surfacing to be healed.

As we've discussed previously, the root chakra represents issues related to the physical world, such as safety and survival. It can also include issues with our physical health, money, food, and home. It affects our relationships as well. We can shut down when we are with other people or isolate as a form of protection. In doing so, we also shut down to ourselves, becoming disconnected from our experiences and our true feelings.

These are all manifestations of a root chakra contraction. The embedded programming is: "It's not safe for me to be in my body." This is often the result of being raised in a chaotic environment with erratic energy being projected onto us. The programming continues, "I might as well absorb this crazy energy, because then I can manage it." That belief system is born out of self-preservation. We take on the discomfort rather than risk others becoming uncomfortable and leaving us or being unavailable. In this way, empaths are taking care of themselves by taking care of others. Empaths have the ability to hold a great deal of other people's energy, but it can be at their own expense.

Another aspect of the root chakra is trust — trust in ourselves, in our family and our community, in humanity and the world. It is also our ability to trust our intuition. Trust can become compromised in childhood when we experience physical abuse, sexual violation, excessive drinking in the home, or mental illness in our primary caregivers. In these situations, your energetic, emotional, and physical boundaries are crossed, your root chakra contracts, and your energy system shuts down to protect you.

Fear and lack of safety create instability in four foundational elements essential for human survival: your family of origin, your home, your health, and your abundance. Safe and loving bonding supports them. We can establish safe and loving bonding as we unwind the root chakra contraction and move deeper into our lower body. Embracing, healing, and releasing the wounds held in the lower chakras, as I've discussed in earlier chapters, are the beginning steps of this process.

Safety and trust are essential for us to feel in order to form attachments with others and the physical world. These qualities reinforce the energy field surrounding our physical body and support healthy boundaries.

That auric energy field mirrors what's happening in your chakras and your entire energy system, including how vibrant or depleted you are. This outer protection is especially important for empathic intuitives. If you are contracted and not feeling safe, or if you have suffered violations to your physical, emotional, or energetic boundaries, your energy field may not be intact. You may have holes, rips, or stagnant energy in your field, or your field may be too soft and permeable. A weakened energy field makes you vulnerable to further violations, such as projections, secrecy, guilt trips, and being yelled at.

Negative or violating energy can cross your auric field and enter your energy body at a primary developmental stage. It then sets up an internalized imprint that it's okay for people to cross into your field. The original negative imprint needs to be repaired or cleared from the root chakra. We cannot go back and change what happened in the past. However, we can shift the energy in our body so that we are no longer carrying these imprints.

Many unconscious beliefs are "rooted" in the root chakra: feeling unlovable or not good enough, lacking a sense of worthiness, experiencing shame and guilt. Even if they are not spoken, the energy of these beliefs is internalized by an empathic intuitive child. This child can develop a very strong monkey mind, an intense inner critic, and a wounded ego. The experiences may not have felt bad or unsafe for the entire childhood, but there may have been situations or dynamics that didn't feel good. When a situation doesn't feel good to a child, the child believes that something is wrong with them. That belief becomes a self-fulfilling prophecy. Once the energetic and emotional template is set in the lower chakras from these patterns, every other experience is run through this filter and validates the child's — or the adult's — core feelings and negative beliefs.

It is important for the empathic intuitive to understand the process of what I call "squashing your self." It begins in the root chakra when you make too much space for others and give them prominence in your energy body. For an empathic intuitive, the paradigm shift begins in the same place — at the core of your energy system. It requires clearing out the energy that caused you to not feel okay being you. As soon as you realize the damaging beliefs exist, you have begun to separate from them. You can observe them happening rather than fully experiencing them. With this newfound objectivity, you become empowered and equipped to move them out of your energetic system.

Grounding will give you the solid foundation you need to

begin to uncover the underlying patterns embedded in your energy system. We need a lot of love and nurturing to reparent the energy in the root chakra so that it will open up and life-force energy can flow freely. An open, grounded root chakra is necessary in order for the rest of the systems to work properly.

JOURNALING EXERCISE

After reading this chapter, contemplate the following questions and respond to them in your journal:

1. What newfound awareness do you have about your root chakra?

2. As you tune in to your root chakra, do you have a sense that you have lived with a contraction born of fear in this power center? If so, what fears do you subconsciously operate from?

3. What unconscious beliefs do you live from in your root chakra area that affect how you operate in the world?

4. What do you need to clear in your root chakra to allow you to have a sense of safety and trust in your-self?

Guided Meditation: Unfurling Your Root Chakra
Audio version available at WendyDeRosa.com/book-meditations

Take a comfortable seat, close your eyes, and deepen your breath. Feel your grounding cord strong and connected from your hips to the center of the earth. Imagine that the earth mother is at the bottom of your grounding cord, offering you security and grounding. She is all-knowing, all-loving, receptive, and nurturing. There isn't anything she can't handle. She loves you unconditionally. She is a mother to all.

As you melt into safety, allow your intuition to guide you to a time period of your life when you could feel the contraction beginning — when you received the awareness that "it's not okay for me to be me."

Take some deep breaths. Let the fear contractions unwind in your root chakra, with the support of the divine earth mother. As they're unwinding, breathe into this red power center at your tailbone. Know that you needed to absorb the energy of your family or society before the age of seven in order to bond with them back then. It's not that absorbing in order to bond was bad, because it wasn't. You needed to belong. But now, you can take responsibility for yourself as an adult. You don't need to continue to operate from this subconscious belief that it's your job to absorb other people's energy.

Once again, take some deep breaths into your root chakra. Recite in your mind or out loud: "Thank you very much. I don't need this energy anymore. I don't need to hold what everybody else thinks and feels about me." Breathe here.

If you were alone after birth, whether because you were hospitalized, in an incubator, or being placed for adoption, deeply exhale the fear and let your root chakra unwind more. Say, "I am releasing this." Down into your grounding cord, let it go.

Keep breathing and releasing. Let go of:

- how much you absorbed
- how much you took on as yours
- feelings of unworthiness
- not being seen
- not being okay

- any other deep-seated beliefs you internalized and made your own

Direct deep breaths into the negative beliefs about yourself. Exhale down your grounding cord as the earth mother below you gathers what you no longer need.

Separate out from your body what is yours and what is not yours. Let that energy continue to unwind, and release it down your grounding cord. Keep breathing here. Your body is a safe place, and your sensitivity is okay.

Very gently now, allow your root chakra to unfurl to a degree that feels comfortable for you. If there's anything else you're holding on to subconsciously here — not being lovable, not being worthy, the belief that you have to embody fear — just keep letting all of that energy go as the mother holds your root chakra and transmits to you safety and love. You are safe in your body. Your Soul can come back into your root chakra. It's okay for you to ground in and connect to your root chakra.

Imagine here and now that your root chakra is the home of your body. It's where you feed yourself. It relates to how you nourish your body, how you take care of your finances, how you are in your environment and in the world. It's your physical home, your wellbeing. It also governs your immune system, your health.

It's time to move back into your root chakra, it's time to make it fully your home. In your lower body, sense how you want to feel when you're at home in your body. Reclaim this area as yours. Take your time breathing into this.

Let your root chakra continue to soften and unfurl, allowing you to build trust and safety in your body. When the root chakra opens, the body slows down. You might get tired. This is good. This means you are grounding into your body.

Let the feelings of safety and trust expand as an energy

down your legs and into your feet. Take a deep seat inside your body. Feel your grounding cord strong and secure.

Is there anything else you need to let go of, any other doubt and fear, anything in the way of you believing that you can reconnect to your sense of self?

Breathe, let go, and feel the power of your grounding.

Let your energy settle here to get stronger. Take more deep breaths and allow a waterfall of light to infuse and brighten your Soul in your body.

Let the light radiate throughout your whole body, expanding all the way around you, beyond your skin and out into your auric field.

From this place of embodiment, know this: No longer are you a victim to the universe and to the energy around you. The protection mechanisms kept you safe for the time in life when you were vulnerable. Thank those protection mechanisms! Thank the disassociation, thank the fight-or-flight response, thank the overeating or whatever repetitive pattern was there for you. These coping mechanisms were helping you during a time when you were lacking power and love in your root chakra. As a spiritually progressing Soul in a human body who is on this earth to continuously grow and evolve, you are safe now, and it's absolutely okay for you to take your power back on behalf of your inner child and fully inhabit your root chakra.

Take your time.

Take a deep breath.

As you are ready, slowly open your eyes.

CHAPTER NINE

The Influence of Trauma on Your Empathic Intuition

Trauma is a psychological and therapeutic term that describes physical, psychological, or emotional injury. Injuries to the body, such as a blow to the brain, the impact of a car accident, or a physical assault, are forms of *physical trauma*. *Psychological trauma* occurs when a frightening or distressing event impacts the psyche. One example of psychological trauma is gaslighting, a manipulative tactic in which a person causes a victim to question the reality of their experience. *Emotional trauma* often coincides with physical and psychological trauma. It is an experience that overwhelms the nervous system and triggers a survival response, such as shutting down, withdrawal, or disassociation. Growing up with neglect, verbal abuse, or alcoholism is likely to cause emotional trauma.

Calming the Trigger Response

I want to pause here for a moment before continuing. Some of the issues that we're discussing can be triggering, especially if you are carrying trauma in your energy body. If you find that you are holding your breath, or feeling tightness in your chest, or your mind is drifting while you are reading, you might be experiencing a trigger response. If so, I encourage you to stop and take a few deep breaths. Feel your body seated in the chair and your feet on the ground; have a sense of being in your body. Sometimes it helps to run your hands up and down your arms and legs. Affirm your energetic anchor in the center of your pillar of light.

I also encourage you to engage in the journaling exercises and guided meditations throughout the book to support you in releasing negative thoughts, imprints, and patterns you may be holding. Energy healing can also be very effective in dealing with trauma. It's important to understand that healing trauma is a path to empowerment — especially for empaths.

How Trauma Affects the Energy Field

We are pure energy. Our thoughts, feelings, and experiences (good and bad) are also made of energy. If an experience was shocking, violating, fearful, confusing, or unsafe, the energy becomes imprinted in the body and stored as trauma. If trauma does not get processed properly at the time, it causes us to develop coping mechanisms, such as addiction or other negative behavioral patterns. While these coping mechanisms may cause harm to ourselves or others, ultimately they form in order to help us survive in the world. The fact that the nervous system takes care of itself when something traumatizing happens is beautiful.

From an energy-healing perspective, trauma is often referred to as a *blockage* because it sits in the energy field of the body. Personally, I think the word *block* is not always appropriate when referring to energy in the body, because it implies that a block can simply be moved out of the way and good energy will begin to flow. While that may be true in some cases, a traumatic imprint isn't a block to be moved but, rather, a doorway to a process of healing, releasing, and finding your power again. As an empath, you may find that empowerment comes from transforming trauma through finding your voice, setting boundaries, and trusting yourself. This deeper healing requires more than just energetically moving a block.

Trauma will form an imprint in a specific chakra on the basis of the qualities of that particular chakra. For example, trauma that relates to safety, such as abandonment, will likely cause the root chakra to close down, resulting in increased fear and a loss of personal power in that area of the body. As another example, if someone experiences violation on an emotional or sexual level, it's likely that the imprint of that trauma will have an effect in the second chakra, which is connected to emotional boundaries, sexuality, and harnessing feminine power. In the energetic body, the history of trauma is most often found in the lower three chakras. As we continue, we will identify other chakras where certain types of trauma are likely to be stored.

Inherited and Collective Trauma in Your Spiritual DNA

When we use energy healing to process trauma, it's not always clear how far back a trauma goes. There could be an experience in this lifetime that felt traumatic, yet it is layered over an experience from a previous lifetime or carried over from your lineage. Sometimes these experiences don't make sense in the context of our personal history. A particular wound brought into this lifetime (from a past life or ancestor) can be just as powerful in creating negative patterns or fears as an experience that just occurred. Indeed, many of us have incarnated in this lifetime to heal the places where these wounds have been inhibiting our power. As we heal, we evolve, and as we evolve, we advance consciousness in the collective. Every new generation brings in new consciousness..

It is important to understand how inherited trauma or imprints are stored in the spiritual DNA of our being. Your spiritual DNA is the Soul's blueprint of your essential self and all you hold. Spiritual DNA carries your Soul's mission, what you are here to accomplish. Because your Soul incarnates through lifetimes, your spiritual DNA carries past-life information, lineage energy, and intergenerational imprinting. The information in your spiritual DNA then becomes imprinted in your physical DNA. From there, your cellular form begins to develop. When viewed from a clairvoyant or intuitive perspective, spiritual DNA looks like the double helix of your physical DNA in the body.

In discussions of energy and patterns, the words *lineage* and *intergenerational* are often used interchangeably; however, they have slightly different meanings. *Lineage energy* broadly encompasses the family line and patterns that are passed down through it, as well as cultural imprints in your spiritual DNA. For example, if your physical DNA test reveals that you have origins in Africa, Asia, and Western Europe, you could be carrying lineage energy from each area of the world that members of your bloodline have lived in. *Intergenerational energy*, on the other hand, encompasses specific unprocessed issues, emotions, traumas, and fears that are passed from one family member to the next. Because these experiences were not resolved, the next generation inherits them as if they are their own. The patterns are then reinforced through experiences in this lifetime and within your current society and culture.

Lineage healing can extend back in time and into cultures where your bloodline is from or your Soul has lived in past lives. Intergenerational healing is more focused and addresses the specific energy and experiences that have been passed down to you from your more recent familial history, often from the generation or two before you. You can recognize this inherited energy because it feels old, stagnant, not quite you, and it typically contains remnants of the behavior of your parents or grandparents. For example, someone who says, "We don't talk about our feelings in my family. My mother didn't, her mother didn't, and so on," likely feels that way because of inherited energy they haven't addressed.

It's especially important for empaths to understand the role and impact of inherited trauma in their healing journey. As empaths, we carry the added historical energy of our ancestors who were unable to express themselves as sensitive, intuitive, spiritual, or empathic beings because it wasn't safe to do so. Simply understanding what is from this lifetime and what you've inherited is empowering in itself and will accelerate your healing process. For example, someone with money issues that include a scarcity mentality, underearning, low self-worth, and self-sabotage could be living a life of lack, fear, and poverty mentality. Let's now say that this person's parents grew up in the Great Depression, lived through oppression, and had very little money, food, or other basic survival needs being met. That inherent parental trauma can be passed down the line. The scarcity and fear of the parents' generation was real for those times. While the times are different now, the person is living that outdated imprint and re-creates the experience in the current life based on what they have inherited. Other traumatic imprints we carry are not from our own lineages but from the collective human experience. During this time of unprecedented division and polarization in the collective, the deeper questions of "How did we get here?" and "Why is this happening?" have thrust the topic of collective trauma into the mainstream. Dialogues on collective trauma and healing humanity are occurring in households and communities, online and around the world.

Collective trauma — such as climate crisis, global pandemics, mass shootings, corrupt politics, or racial and gender-based violence — can also trigger one's personal trauma. These unprecedented times present an unprecedented opportunity to heal, both personally and collectively. Healing trauma has become a dominant aspect of the therapeutic process. Now we are being called to address trauma beyond counseling. By integrating therapeutic tools with energy healing techniques, we are able to get underneath the symptoms and patterns we experience in the body and facilitate healing at the deepest level.

Honoring the Trauma-Healing Process

While energy healing has always addressed processing traumatic energetic imprints in the body, it hasn't always properly identified trauma. For many years, energy healing traditions referred to trauma by other terms, such as *karma, karmic wounds, intergenerational wounds, past-life wounds,* and *samskaras* (scars). Today, in spiritual circles, trauma is sometimes misidentified as "negativity" or "negative energy," and people with unprocessed trauma are sometimes given judgmental labels, such as "energy vampire" or "crazy."

"Spiritual" teachings that minimize, dismiss, or ignore the role of processing trauma in one's personal growth create a polarity between light and dark, preventing a holistic experience of one's humanity. This binary approach hinders one's ability to be fully present in their life and relationships. Such denial also creates a *shadow*, an aspect that is suppressed, is hidden, or we don't want to admit having. If we're locked into the binary approach, we are forced into being good or bad, right or wrong, and, again, light or dark. The shadow exists unconsciously and undermines our ability to move forward. Such a paradigm is the opposite of a holistic experience of one's humanity.

The healing process requires more than putting a bubble of light around yourself and going out into the world. While the bubble of light can be temporary support, it won't protect you from having negative feelings, or getting triggered, or needing to engage in difficult conversations. True protection comes from healing the wounds, specifically those held in your first three chakras, so that you can express more of your true light and power and strengthen your empathic boundaries. When empaths walk in the world fully embodied, they become powerful truth tellers and models for empathy.

It can be confusing for empaths to identify whether they are feeling someone else's energy or their own, especially when they carry unprocessed traumas that get triggered. Based on my own personal life and my experience as a healer, I can tell you that it is not always someone else's energy. If you are triggered, pause and ask yourself the question "What is mine in this?" Sit quietly, taking the position of an observer, and inquire what is within you that is being triggered. There is always going to be something for you to see about your own energy.

JOURNALING EXERCISE

Have you noticed any body responses as you read this chapter? Take some time to reflect on them now by answering the following questions in your journal:

1. When you tune in to your lower chakras, can you identify any imprints you are holding in your lower body that may have come through your lineage?
2. Think back on the collective traumas that have occurred in your lifetime. As you've experienced some of these collective traumas, have there been any personal traumas or imprints that have come into your awareness?
3. What support do you have in place or need to seek in order to process past experiences that were hurtful?
4. In what ways can you prioritize the healing of unprocessed trauma?

Guided Meditation: Loving Your Inner Child
Audio version available at WendyDeRosa.com/book-meditations

Know that you are human, and you have the strength and the power to heal your past. This meditation is an invitation to go easy and love yourself more.

Take a comfortable seat and close your eyes. Begin breathing deeply into your body. Bring your awareness to your lower belly. Seated in the center of your lower belly, see an image of your inner child. Your inner child is an aspect of your emotional needs, and they know what you require on an emotional level to feel safe and secure. Your inner child is also an aspect of your intuition. Listening to your inner child's wisdom helps you meet your emotional needs.

Take some deep breaths and feel into your inner child. What do they look like? Does your inner child look content? Or does your inner child feel upset or scared? Without any judgment of your inner child's experience, let your inner child know that you are present, that you see them, and that you're going to give them your attention right now.

Your inner child might be carrying some feelings about the past, about experiences that were out of their control. Your inner child may have something to say or emotions to express about those experiences.

Your only job in this moment is to love your inner child as they are. Love your inner child through the feelings of hurt, the feelings of joy, the feelings of fear, or any other feelings that your inner child may be having.

Allow your inner child to sit on your lap. Hold your inner child close and let this part of you recover, relax, and feel safe. This restoration is so powerful for the part of you that is still seeking safety and repair from the past.

Look your inner child in the eye. See this beautiful, bright essence that lives inside you and is the spark of your prevailing spirit. The more you connect to your inner child, the more connected you are to your authentic Self and your truth.

Take as much time as you need to be here with your inner child on your lap, embraced in your arms and loved. Allow your mind to soften, your heart to soften, your nervous system to soften, and an inner bond to form between you and your inner child. Breathe here.

Know that this bond is a connection you can return to over and over again. Know this as a felt sense in your body.

Spend a few moments here in silence. Breathe. Take as much time as you need.

As you are ready, slowly open your eyes.

CHAPTER TEN

How Fear and Lack Can Block Your Empathic Intuition

In chapter 8, we explored root chakra contraction as a response to feeling unsafe in early childhood. This fear response also happens when we feel threatened, fearful, or lacking as adults, causing us to repeat patterns of hypervigilance and disconnection from our own body. The root chakra contraction begins a cycle of more fear and sense of lack, more contraction, then even more feelings of fear and lack. As with other types of trauma we've been exploring, the energy of fear and lack may originate in early childhood, inherent wounds, or fear-based beliefs. And of course, as we've been discussing, these subconscious patterns are particularly destabilizing for empaths and make it difficult to hold energetic boundaries in the world.

Fear is a subconscious emotion. We don't normally *feel* it in the root chakra or tailbone area of the body, but we unconsciously operate from fear in that part of the body and form coping mechanisms to deal with it. Fear in and of itself is not a problem. In its healthy form, it keeps us safe and protected. Where it becomes a problem is when no repair or comfort is provided or when it escalates to terror, which then becomes imprinted in your sensitive energy body.

As human beings, we can be taught a healthy fear response. We can learn to recognize appropriate fear and to listen to it. Subconscious fears and fear-based beliefs are different. What was originally intended to be a signal for our protection becomes a way of being in the world. Fear of being criticized, disliked, and abandoned creates imprints that become so deeply embedded within us, we form false beliefs about who we are, such as "I am not worthy" or "It's not okay to be me." We develop a distorted lens through which we see the world.

For an empath who is operating from a foundation of subconscious fear, the world is never going to feel like a safe place to be. Sensitive beings internalize "This feels wrong" as "Something's wrong *with me.*" Fear of not being okay, worthy, or enough forms ingrained patterns, false beliefs that ultimately become self-fulfilling prophecies as we create and re-create situations that reinforce them. As we've discussed earlier, this fear-based way of living causes us to vacate the lower chakras, leaving us susceptible to other people's energies and vulnerable to taking on other people's fears in those areas. It can be difficult to let go of certain fears when they stem from lack, such as from being deprived of love. How can you release something that you didn't have to begin with? In these instances, healing comes from nurturing the areas where you experienced emotional and energetic deprivation. Directing your awareness to these areas can help you to reclaim your power and embody the places where you hold patterns of abandonment by caregivers and others responsible for your wellbeing. We can begin to comfort our inner child and fulfill the needs that were not met earlier in life.

When we speak of lack, we often think of a lack of resources, such as money. Lack on an energetic level means an absence or a void. Some of the areas where energetic lack manifests in the physical realm are finances (from poverty to underearning to excessive spending); home; relationships; and emotional, mental, and physical health (more about that in a moment).

Fear and trauma can be imprinted in our energy bodies, especially in the lower chakras, when in early life we experience a lack of any of these:

being seen	safety
belonging	security
comfort	sense of self
connection	sustenance
faith	trust in others
love	trust in self
money	validation
presence in the body	worthiness

These forms of lack, along with many others, can cause you to become ungrounded and detached from your physical body. That disembodiment, a disconnection from the vital earth energy (which, as we know, is harnessed in the root chakra), can lead to health issues such as:

addictions	chronic fatigue
allergies	chronic pain
anxiety and panic	eating disorders
disorders	fibromyalgia
asthma or bronchitis	insomnia and other sleep
autoimmune diseases	conditions
bone density loss	irritable bowel syndrome

lymph system problems	obsessive-compulsive
mental fog and inability	behavior
to focus	sexual and reproductive
	health problems

Empaths, highly sensitive people, and intuitives often share a number of the physical symptoms listed above, especially chronic fatigue. It is important to note that if you are experiencing any of these symptoms, you may need to be treated by a medical practitioner. In addition, understanding the energetic components underlying or contributing to your health condition can support and accelerate your healing.

The energy you're carrying in your lower chakras, and in the root chakra specifically, informs the health of your other power centers and your overall health at a cellular level. When you are experiencing lack, your root chakra may be sending a signal to the rest of your energy system that there isn't enough vital life-force energy available to function properly.

Lack of love in the root chakra is often the primary issue underlying many of these health conditions. The root chakra governs your physical form; therefore, if you are deprived of love at the level of the root chakra, you are deprived of the vitality you need for wellness. When you are deprived of embodied love, insufficient life-force energy moves through the physical body. The lack of love often translates "Who I am is not enough" into "not enough" of what your body needs to be optimally healthy.

You might be wondering, "What if I have love in the other chakras? Can't I thrive and be empowered?" Unfortunately, while you might be able to thrive in some areas of life, such as business, you won't be truly empowered until you address the lack in your root chakra. This is because the root chakra plays a key role in the energetic body, which is to provide vital sustenance to your human form and support your connection to the earth. You could have love in every other power center and still not feel worthy. You could embody love in your heart chakra and still feel poor and deprived in spirit.

How to Heal Root Chakra Contractions Caused by Fear and Lack

So how do you work with this kind of deprivation? Can you just close your eyes and visualize filling your root chakra with love? That might work for some people. However, others meet the idea of allowing love into the root chakra area of their body with resistance. Shifting energy in this area may cause them to bump up against feelings that have been embedded there for protection. When visualizing energy or working with intentions is not enough, here are some other healing methods to consider.

Grounding

Grounding, as we've discussed, is a primary way to connect to your root chakra. Implementing some tools or the meditation offered in chapter 5 can be a supportive way to ground the energy in your body. Grounding energetically means that you connect not only to your body and the earth but also to your truth, emotions, intuition, safety, and trust. The qualities of grounding are the opposite of fear, which is why it is wise to take a moment to ground yourself whenever you feel fear or when you embark on healing any aspect of yourself. Grounding also helps you connect with the inherent energy you are holding in your root chakra and lower body.

Inner Child Bonding

When you are dealing with any of your lower chakras, keep in mind that this area of the body represents early childhood development. You're not talking to your adult self. You're talking to your inner child. The inner child is intimately linked to your intuition. It is also the part of you that relates to your most basic physical and emotional needs.

If your root chakra has been wounded by a lack of love and safety, you may need to redefine your concept of what love really is. You can do this by slowly and gently building a relationship of trust with your inner child consciousness. You can assure your inner child that it is now safe for you to reclaim this area of your body and make it your home. Once you begin to feel safe in this area, the rest of the body will be supported to heal. And when your inner child begins to feel safe here, you can feel at home anywhere, because home is in your body.

Reclaiming Self-Love

Another way to heal lack in the root chakra is to feel love as an innate physical essence in your body. Like attracts like. So if you maintain a vibration of unworthiness and lack, the universe matches that energy, and so do other people. Once you accept that you are wholly worthy of love and respect, you can shift this vibration for good. You can create a new imprint of love and being loved at an energetic level.

Reclaiming self-love and a sense of self in the root chakra is an act of empowerment. Yet, as you return to your root chakra domain, feelings from childhood might arise: grief for what you didn't receive, pain for what happened to you, or an awareness of joy you had forgotten. Grounding into the root chakra is not always comfortable initially. To some people it will feel really good and very grounding. For others, it might stir feelings of fatigue, restlessness, being unsettled, and a desire to escape, withdraw, or shut down. Remember that emotions are not negative; they are human. Tears can be cleansing, anger can be purifying, discomfort can be the catalyst for you to come back into alignment.

Removing Blindfolds

When the blindfolds come off and we see what we've been subconsciously carrying, we begin to transform at the root chakra level. Spiritual growth is not about moving your conscious awareness higher, up and out of your body. It's about going deeper into the Soul's essence in the center of your being, rooted in your human experience. We are here to live on this earth as spiritual beings, connected to both the physical realm and the spirit realm. This is how we will leave a powerful footprint and a lasting legacy on our planet. Blindfolds and other protection mechanisms that have kept us safe will dissolve as we pivot and embrace the energy and experiences we have spent much of our lifetime avoiding.

Understanding and Appreciating
Your Protection Mechanisms

Feelings of shame, disassociation, overactive fight-flight-freeze responses, and more have kept you from fully embodying your lower chakras. Recognizing that these responses are your energy body's protection mechanisms, as well as your spirit's way of keeping you safe, is essential for your healing as an empath. As part of the healing process, it's important to explore why your energy body and spirit were protecting you and what they were protecting you from. Another step in the healing process is to thank them for responding in this way and so lovingly caring for you.

Healing Your Personal Conditioning Shifts the Collective

It's not easy work to unpack all that we are holding in the root chakra, because we carry so many layers there. Human existence is based on multiple layers of conditioning that have allowed us to survive. These layers are imprinted in our energetic system, forming embedded patterns. They are as intricate as they are deep and can span multiple lifetimes. Over time, they become dense and thick, forging and reinforcing our attitudes and mental constructs. They shape our worldview, self-perceptions, and ego. While they form to help us survive, they ultimately keep us confined. We become disconnected from our divine Self. They become the painful patterns that we seek to unravel on our path of transformation. Our spiritual path becomes a process of remembering the true nature of who we are as a Soul in this body.

The system we exist in at this time was built on years of conditioning and layers of beliefs rooted in inequality and injustice. They, too, started as a form of protection from both real and imagined fears about survival. Over time, this system has been reinforced and made worse by greed, overindulgence, and instant gratification.

While we express outrage at racial, economic, environmental, and social injustices today — and we should! — the most impactful change we can create is within ourselves. Change is possible through the work we are doing right now.

As we heal the layers of imprints within us, as we release beliefs and lifetimes of patterns, we are chipping away at these layers in the collective as well. Inherited beliefs about ourselves and the world that contribute to the suppression of our true being are the same mechanisms that contribute to the oppression of others. These ingrained beliefs are at the basis of the chaos we are witnessing today in our families, in our communities, and in the world. They also hold the keys to healing our families, our communities, and our world.

There Are Always More Layers — and It's a Good Thing!

I have spent the majority of my life healing from childhood struggles, uncovering shadow elements within myself through energy healing, therapy, yoga, singing, and a number of other modalities. My early life was marked by deprivation and the shame, fear, and lack that come with it. I have not felt "privileged," because so much of my life has been shaped by striving and surviving, not having enough, and not being enough. This poverty mindset has touched every area of my life. It has also opened a deep path of healing and transformation.

As the awareness of deeply embedded racism in society and culture, here in the United States and around the world, has come to the forefront of our collective consciousness, I have found myself confronted with my own ideas, prejudices, and blind spots. I have a multicultural background, I am in a biracial relationship, and I have a biracial child. These, combined with my childhood mindset and worldview that privilege was how other people lived, have led me to a profound growth edge. Authentic conversations with my husband, hearing him share his everyday experiences as a man of color, and listening to women of color have led me to a newfound realization about my part in systemic racism. This crisis of consciousness has thrust me into a deeper level of processing and healing.

When I began to work through the newly revealed layers and increase my awareness of deeply embedded patterns, I uncovered privilege in my life that came from simply being born white. As I dug deeper and felt into what the black girls were likely feeling in my classes when they sat in the back row, I was overcome with shame and flooded with awareness about racism in my childhood. While I knew it was wrong back then, this time I felt what they must have felt. I felt sick to my stomach that I had played a part in that normalized segregation. I began to unravel conflicted feelings over the Fourth of July and Thanksgiving, coming to see these "holidays" as celebrations of dysfunction and devastation. I realized that my privilege was my ability to keep a blindfold on and the discomfort at bay. My own experiences of lack and dysfunction were distractions from the real pain that comes from confronting these realities. My privilege enabled me to hide from the truth.

For me, processing these imprints has also meant healing another layer of my tendency to be overly empathic, to not stand in my power, and to back away from confronting uncomfortable or inconvenient truths. Like many white people in our society, I had adopted innate ways of existing that reflected the collective denial of truth, as leaders gaslighted those who tried to share any contrary experience. I have had to come to terms with my participation in a system that is unequal and unjust to others. I have had to stop covering up my feelings and to take more responsibility for my implicit bias.

If you are a person of color who identifies as an empath, you may be carrying additional imprints that have been projected upon you. The fear held in your root chakra originates from the entire history of racial and cultural oppression that you experience. Owning your anger, grief, and outrage and reclaiming your power in this area of your body are essential for your healing. However, the issue of racism is a collective issue held in the lower chakras, and therefore a change in collective consciousness is needed for full healing.

Racial injustice is not the burden of one group or another to heal. The concept of "race" itself is a social construct and does not account for the abundant genetic diversity in humans. The first step in healing racial injustice is to recognize it as rooted in power imbalances that we all participate in, consciously and unconsciously. No one wants to admit they have biases; however, this ignores the systems and structures in society that perpetuate inequality and impact every area of our lives. I believe we are being called to a time of deep reconciliation — both within ourselves and with one another.

White people, often of Western European descent, have a crucial role to play in shifting the power imbalances of oppression. I feel it is important to address racism because the power imbalances that give way to racism (as well as all injustice) stem from wounds held in the root chakra, a central topic of discussion throughout this book. As I mentioned earlier, the root chakra is the power center that holds our human existence issues, the foundational feelings of belonging and safety (or lack thereof) in the human experience. While racial issues affect other chakras, because they divide humanity, they most directly affect the root chakra. As we empaths find our power and heal, we play a part in the rise of consciousness; we must include healing the pain of racism in deep consciousness work. People with unconscious bias hold beliefs that are often passed off as "spiritual," such as "I don't see color" and "We are all one," which inadvertently minimize and dismiss the very real suffering that people of color have lived through and continue to live with. True allyship is hearing, seeing, and validating the experiences that people of color are sharing. Eradicating racial inequality is not to be viewed as solely work of world leaders and legislators; it is our work to do in this lifetime — individually and collectively.

Uncovering these layers involves building awareness and engaging in a process of humble self-inquiry, which are important actions for white people. Reading, exploring racial issues in honest conversation with others, and journaling are first steps in this discovery process. Parallel contemplative practices, such as exploring the history of racism in your country or family and tracing memories of living in the blind spot of systemic racism, are essential for uncovering the patterns that are operating in you on a subconscious level. Through conscious exploration accompanied by energy healing, we can shift the energy we're carrying and create new imprints for future generations. Transformation *is* possible — in ourselves and in the collective.

JOURNALING EXERCISE

Take a moment, breathe, and respond to these journal prompts:

1. What is the story of fear and lack in your root chakra?

2. How did fear and lack play out in your family lineage? Did your mother and/or father's side of the family carry patterns of fear and lack?

3. How do fear and lack influence your beliefs about yourself, your behaviors, and/or your choices?
4. What energy did you marinate in as a child that contributed to a root chakra contraction?
5. What limiting beliefs did you internalize and believe about yourself?
6. What beliefs based in fear or lack are you letting go of?
7. What new, empowered beliefs are you claiming?
8. What came up for you when addressing race, white privilege, and bias as part of root chakra healing?

If it supports you, continue journaling on what is coming up for you after reading this chapter. If this work becomes more than you can do on your own, it may be a good time to reach out to a healer, therapist, or other qualified practitioner for support.

Guided Meditation: Healing Fear and Lack
Audio version available at WendyDeRosa.com/book-meditations

Take a comfortable seat. Breathe and settle into your body.

Take some deep breaths. Feel your strong and secure grounding cord connected from your hips to the center of the earth, joining you to the earth mother. Return to the awareness of the safe, all-knowing, all-loving presence of the earth mother. You've visited your root chakra before. Now you will go a bit deeper.

Allow your root chakra to soften. Breathe into fears stored here. Your intuition will help guide you to inherited or subconscious fears that contribute a feeling that you are lacking, are not good enough, or never have enough. Preverbally, maybe in the womb, maybe later in your adolescence or in your child-hood, you internalized these feelings. As a result, you may have felt unworthy, insecure, and diminished on an emotional and/or physical level.

Breathe deeply down into your root chakra. Let the fears unwind.

Release the energy you needed to absorb in order to bond to the adults in your life or live in the family system that may not serve you now. Choose to let it go.

It's not that absorbing for bonding purposes was bad, be-cause it wasn't. But where you are in your life now, you can take responsibility for yourself on a whole new level. You don't need to operate from subconscious beliefs that you are not worthy of having or should fear having.

Take more deep breaths into your root chakra, and as you release, recite: "Thank you. I don't need this energy anymore. I don't need to keep carrying innate fear and lack from my family. I choose abundance and am teaching myself now that it's okay for me to have."

Send some deep breaths into the negative beliefs about yourself. Exhale down your grounding cord. The divine mother is below you, unwinding the energy held at your root chakra. Keep breathing as you tune in to what your root chakra is holding.

Let go of the inherited or present-day pain of not being enough. Take your time and breathe deeply.

Let go and allow the feeling of safety to be restored at your root chakra.

Imagine that the flower of your root chakra is planted in fertile soil and that you are watering that flower. Imagine that the water is the purest love, filled with medicine that your root chakra needs to give you a new foundation.

Marinate in this love in your root chakra. Breathe and allow this power center to soak up pure, grounded, abundant love. It may be a different quality of energy than you received in your youth. It's a quality of energy that your Soul needs now.

Breathe.

Allow the feeling of abundance to radiate throughout your being. Feel your body glow. Let the cells in your body absorb this new, abundant love.

Affirm for yourself now: "I live in the present moment, receiving myself and my worth. I trust that it is okay for me to have comfort, peace, love, safety, and belonging. I am enough."

Feel your grounding cord grow strong. Let the light radiate throughout your whole body, expanding all the way around you, beyond your skin, brightening the auric field that encircles your being.

May you radiate from your innate worth and feel empowered in your body.

CHAPTER ELEVEN

Reconnect with Your Emotional Center and Tap into the Power of the Feminine

Your emotional center, your empathic intuition, and your feminine power (whether you are male or female or non-binary) all operate from the same power center in the body: the second chakra. Located in the pelvis, it is one of the most delicate and sensitive power centers of the body. The innate healing power of your empathic intuition is rooted in your second chakra. For empaths, this is your power center that is deeply in tune with the flow of life, the felt and the unspoken.

In Sanskrit, the second chakra is the Svadhisthana chakra, which means "one's own dwelling." Your second chakra holds a vast history containing your emotional experiences, relationships, and how attuned you are with the world around you. The Svadhisthana chakra is connected to your creativity, sexuality, sensuality, sweetness, playfulness, and vulnerability. It is your energetic center for going with the flow, connecting to your divine nature, and feeling the full spectrum of your emotions. It is the creation center for mothering, birthing, and new beginnings.

These powers are strengths. However, historically they have not been valued by Western patriarchal cultures and societies. They have been seen as weaknesses or something to hide. Aspects of the feminine (in all genders) have been devalued. As a result, the second chakra has been the target of oppression in the public sphere. We, in turn, have internalized these beliefs and suppressed our own gifts and their expression in others. As we are birthing a new era of consciousness that values truth, this power center will no longer remain oppressed — nor will the empath.

The empathic nature in the body is the power of the feminine. Richness, beauty, innocence, and softness are innate in the feminine, all qualities that connect an empath to their emotional self. As well, injuries to the feminine have been passed down through our spiritual DNA and intergenerationally. The empath has an important role to play in transforming these wounds and reclaiming all aspects of feminine power in themselves and in the world. We begin the path to healing and wholeness by understanding and addressing history. As with the process of healing the root chakra, we explore what we are carrying and then what we have been cocreating in the collective.

Throughout Western history, expressing the feminine has had its consequences regardless of what body one is in. Sometimes these consequences have been severe. Fear of the feminine has caused society to cast healers as charlatans, powerful women as witches or bitches, and emotional men and women as weak. Sexuality has been dominated by the patriarchy, creating a denigration, devaluing, and abuse of healthy sexuality, as well as the objectification and oppression of women. In the same vein, creative expression is often undervalued in industrialized society, and artists are viewed as frivolous.

Culturally we are often trained out of feeling emotions, so we learn to suppress and ignore them. In response, we experience shame over having emotions. This shame forms another layer that blocks us from our second chakra power and imprints negative patterns within our entire energy body.

Over time, the emotional part of our being can't stay suppressed any longer. It will seek outlets by which to express itself — for example, overeating, overspending, addictions, midlife crises, extramarital affairs, and so on. Unexpressed feelings can explode as intense reactions, including anger and rage.

Energetic systems often show a split between the upper and lower body. The most common source of this split is shame. Because of the toxic history associated with the lower half of the body, we have an innate sense that we should disassociate ourselves from it — and therefore from the power that exists in our lower chakras.

Shame informs our identity, promoting the idea that we are inherently bad and wrong. Shame is what motivates us to abide by society's rules, as corrupt as they may be, in order to belong and to receive love. Shame comes through your spiritual DNA as deeply embedded imprints that can last lifetimes. It's the suppression of your second chakra power that was passed on through both your maternal and your paternal lineages. Because this imprinting is at a Soul level, patterns are also carried from past lives into this lifetime.

Now, the feminine is rising: individuals are talking about it, national conversations are happening, and media feeds are filled with it. The feminine aspect of being is making its presence known. No matter what body you inhabit, your true voice can no longer stay suppressed, and your desire for freedom of expression is urging you to bring forward your *full* physical, sexual, emotional, and spiritual aspects.

The power of the second chakra is in your ability to subtly attune to your feelings. The key is to pause, ground into your body, and connect with your inner child and with nature. It's about deeply listening to what your second chakra has to express and affirming your connection to your divine Self.

It's important for empaths to recognize and to feel their emotions. Without this process, you will not know what emotions are yours and what emotions you are taking on from others. This is deep Soul work. Boundaries have been crossed, and those violations have left their energetic patterns on your second chakra. You likely have feelings about these patterns: grief and loss from being shut down, from not having access to your power sooner. Now it is safe for you to have the emotions that you were unable to feel and process earlier.

When you feel your feelings, you embody them. To be seated in the center of your emotional self means that you are anchored in the center of your second chakra and powerfully grounded into your truth, your power, and your divine being. Your sensitivity means you are in tune with the subtle. Through your second chakra, you sense what's happening beneath the surface. You walk into a room and are instantly aware of all the energy there and what is happening on a nonverbal level. Second chakra power is like a divining rod for what's true, the ability to separate truth from falsehoods.

If our second chakra becomes congested with shame, unprocessed emotions, and a sense of unworthiness, we are not able to sit powerfully in this area of our body or connect to our deeper knowing. Access to our deeper knowing supports our empathic intuition. Empathic intuition allows us to feel what's happening in the world, and the knowing sense helps us stay grounded and connected to how we feel.

When we lose touch with our emotions, we are no longer connected to the feelings that are occurring in our lower body. This unexpressed energy becomes part of our shadow. It's what others might perceive in us or coming from us, but because it's in our shadow, we are either unwilling or unable to recognize it ourselves.

One way we attempt to have our survival and emotional needs met is through hypervigilance. We are constantly scanning the room and the energy of our caregivers for cues on how we should behave. We then take care of those around us to keep ourselves safe. For example, if we perceive a person is angry, we might try to soothe them. When our second chakra is compromised, this action comes from a survival-based need rather than from compassion: "I need to calm them down so that I will be safe and they will love me."

In this way, you learn at a young age to be responsible for the negative feelings of others being projected on or around you. They aren't your emotions; however, as a sensitive child you absorb and internalize them. Once internalized, the feelings merge with your own, and it is difficult to know where your energetic and emotional body ends and others' begin. This makes it virtually impossible to have and hold clear boundaries, as children and as adults.

To break these patterns involves both owning and embodying your energy, discerning what is yours and what is the property of others. It also means tolerating other people having emotions. Your willingness to sit in the discomfort that their emotions produce and not take them on is in direct proportion to your ability to have and maintain healthy boundaries.

You were likely raised in an environment where it was normal to take on the energy and emotions of others. This is why it is uncomfortable to allow others to express their feelings and not take care of them. Be gentle with yourself. You are unwinding years (and lifetimes) of patterns.

Your empathy for others is natural and good. When your pure empathy shifts into being overempathy toward other people, however, it becomes problematic. If you were overly responsible for a parent's wellbeing, then to say no or to do something purely for yourself would likely leave you feeling selfish or guilty. You find yourself in a bind: you feel resentful taking care of them out of a sense of obligation, but you also can't take care of yourself for fear of losing connection or love.

We are not able to resolve these patterns of guilt until we embody our lower chakras and connect to our true Self — especially in the second chakra. When you feel embodied, present, safe, and grounded in who you are, feelings of guilt will subside. You will likely still feel guilt sometimes, as it is a natural human emotion. Healthy guilt serves as an alert when we're off-center and need to be brought back to our moral compass.

When we are unable to heal and release these imprints, we are likely to end up in codependent relationships or acting out in ways that alienate others. These patterns can also manifest in our work life — for example, by causing us to overwork or underearn.

What makes these patterns compelling is really that they feel good (at first). It feels good to be taken care of, and we feel good taking care of others. Taking care of people gives us a sense of purpose. Over time, however, if the only way we bond with others is through taking care of them energetically, emotionally, physically, and spiritually, we limit access to other parts of ourselves.

Awareness of these patterns can take time to cultivate. It takes patience and bravery to understand the impact of being raised in an environment where other people's energy and emotions were projected onto you. This is not a process you need to work out with your family of origin. In fact, you may find it best to take a break from physical contact while you untangle your feelings and energy. And remember, these patterns have likely been with you for lifetimes. Spending time with your inner child, nurturing them, and giving them your uninterrupted attention can help you heal the patterns for yourself and for the next generation.

Your inner child is essential in your healing process. Ultimately, this is who you are reparenting. Your inner child needs affirmation that it wasn't okay that so much responsibility was put on them at such a young age. You need to recognize the feelings and intuition of your inner child and let them know that they're safe to feel their emotions. Give yourself the time and space to express your emotions and to be honest with yourself about how you feel. The negative patterns are not just in your head, and they are not in some vague portal we call the past. They are literally in your lower body.

At the end of this chapter, you have access to a guided practice for clearing, healing, and grounding your emotional center. Here is an additional short meditation that you can also use in your contemplative practice.

Begin by taking a deep breath into your second chakra. As you exhale, release the energy that is blocked in your lower body. Continue to breathe deeply into this area of your body and sit for a moment, allowing this part of your body to just breathe. Take your time in releasing this energy when you exhale.

Drop deeper into your lower body, your second chakra, and release energy down your grounding cord to the center of the earth. As you release energy, you make room for yourself to come more fully into this space. Release what is not yours or is no longer serving you. Ground deeply into this space with your energy and your presence.

As you reclaim the space of your second chakra, affirm that you are safe. Affirm your feelings that are arising. Embrace the shame, guilt, and resentment. Bless and release these emotions and thank them for their service in alerting you to what is no longer in alignment with you and your purpose.

A lot of emotions might emerge at the same time, including sadness and grief. These emotions can feel overwhelming at first. If you can, stay with the waves of emotion and allow them to wash over you. Keep breathing. Keep releasing.

If this process becomes too much to do on your own, seek out the aid of a trusted friend or professional. Allow yourself to receive this loving-kindness for all that you are and this support for processing all that you have been holding.

JOURNALING EXERCISE

What has come to your awareness through reading this chapter? Take a moment, breathe, and let the words flow in response to the following questions:

1. How were you taught or not taught to have your emotions?
2. What has been your relationship to your emotions?
3. What is your relationship to your emotions now?

4. What is your experience of shame and guilt?
5. Describe what sitting in your emotional center and power could look like for you.
6. In what ways can you take care of yourself emotionally?

* * *

Guided Meditation: Seat Yourself in Your Emotional Center
Audio version available at WendyDeRosa.com/book-meditations

* * *

Take a comfortable seat and breathe deeply. Feel your grounding cord connected from your hips to the center of the earth. Fill your tailbone and root chakra area with a sense of your presence. Slow down your breath. Slow down your mind. Breathe deeply.

Imagine a throne in the center of your second chakra; you are the regal presence seated there. You can see yourself as a king or queen embodying your feminine essence.

Call all your emotional energy back to you, including any emotions that you've projected onto others. You are taking responsibility for your effect on others now. In any way that you've projected anger, blame, shame, or negativity, call that energy back.

Inhale it back into your body and exhale it down your grounding cord, releasing it to the earth, where it will be transformed as renewed life-force energy. Repeat for as long as you need to.

Then, mentally apologize to all the people whom you may have hurt unconsciously because you did not know what to do with the wounds you were feeling, wounds that perhaps needed an outlet to express themselves.

Breathe.

Ask for forgiveness. Ask for forgiveness from yourself first. Then ask for forgiveness from a higher power for any way that you acted out from hurt that you were feeling. Forgive yourself. Forgive your teenage self, your twenty-something self, your thirty-something self, and so on.

Forgive the parts of you that were in bits and pieces and not whole. And call all of you back into your body and into wholeness. Become wholesome in this moment.

Breathe.

Now send everybody back to their own bodies. Let their inner children call them back so that you no longer take care of lost parts of them. Visualize their higher Self grounding into their own body and taking responsibility for their lives and their emotions. Lay their energy at their feet so they may pick up the pieces and become whole too. Leave it. It's not for you to track. You can be okay with their discomfort, because through discomfort we grow.

Come back to the sanctuary in the center of your second chakra. Design it, create it. Visualize your throne and feel it. It can be regal and strong, like that of a warrior goddess, or it can be soft and plush, like green grass and the comforts of nature. It's your creation, where you are in tune with yourself and the sensual world around you. Life desensitized you from the bounty of this power center. In this moment, give yourself full permission to embody your Self here in your second chakra.

Breathe.

You are not alone here. The light of unity, love, and grace joins you here. It weaves itself through your organs and your fascia. It purifies what was toxic to your body and dissolves it. It cleanses you and loves you just as you are. It helps you remember the true you. The more time you make space for it, the more of you you'll remember.

Bathe here in divine grace. Let this light of divinity fill your second chakra region and shower you in beauty and divinity. Focus on the love and the light in this area as you breathe, and let the wounds and contractions shaking your body have expression. Then let them go.

Breathe here.

You are reclaiming your throne. You are purifying a room in your holy house. It's time for you to make a home here. Move in, reclaim, soften, and melt into this space. Create whatever protection you need around your domain in order to have the discernment and privacy that will support you in being in your power. Create it in your mind's eye, not from fear, but from self-respect and personal responsibility for your energy.

Let this domain in your second chakra be a place where your energy body takes the precious time it needs to feel and to be you. You may need to visit this area of your body often until something clicks. Once may not be enough, twice may not be enough. Follow your intuition as it tells you what you need.

Bathe here in the light of your deep divine essence and let it renew you. No matter what anyone else needs around you, this is your throne of personal responsibility, emotional permission, and the value of your powerfully emerging divine feminine.

Be here and breathe here as long as you need to, until you feel complete.

CHAPTER TWELVE

Healing the Wounded Feminine and the Wounded Masculine

D o you find yourself wondering about the narcissists in
your life? And what you've done to attract them? If
so, you're not alone. This is a common question for empaths
to ask.

It is important to explore this dynamic in depth because
it highlights the impact of inherited patriarchy, the wounded
masculine, the wounded feminine, and codependent patterns
that reside as unconscious layers in the pelvic region of our
body. A deeper examination also sheds light on the shifts taking place in the world with regard to both feminine and empathic power.

A crucial step in this process is to examine the shadow
influence of these dynamics and understand how they under-
mine your ability to move forward on your path, in your spiritual growth, in your life's work, in your relationships, and
more. As we've seen before, the inherent patterns are not just
in you, your family, or the collective. They're patterns that

have been passed down through generations and replayed over and over throughout history.

This deep work brings our focus to the second chakra, a relationship power center, and to our empathic intuition, which plays out in our relationships with others. Just as a reminder, when empaths feel the energy of others, they will inherently want to take care of any energy that makes them feel ungrounded. That tendency feeds the energetic interplay between the narcissist and the empath and the deep unmet needs that attract them to each other.

Though I'm not a clinician, the experience I share with you is based on my work as an intuitive healer, what I have observed through my case studies with clients, and what they have shared with me. In the collective and in the media I am seeing more and more conversations about narcissists, so it's important to address their dynamic as it relates to empaths. This is one more layer of the second chakra to be explored, especially if you have narcissists in your life! If appropriate, this layer can then be processed and healed.

Narcissism occurs on a spectrum. At one end of the spectrum is clinical narcissism. The mark of clinical narcissism is the narcissist's inability to believe there is anything wrong with them. At the other end of the spectrum, a person can exhibit narcissistic tendencies from time to time when they're under stress, when they feel imbalanced, or when they are extremely self-focused. Those who are raised by narcissists may carry narcissistic tendencies. If they are able to work with a therapist and receive support, they're usually able to transform these tendencies and to live a healthy, balanced life.

Empaths and narcissists have a seemingly magnetic attraction to each other. Empaths have an innate desire to caretake others, and in an unhealthy state, they can do so to the point where they lose their center. In such a vulnerable state, they may easily be in relationship with a narcissist whose ego is inflated by their care and attention but who also exerts power and control over them.

Both the unhealthy empath and the narcissist have difficulty owning their own emotional center and being connected to their authentic Self. Together they form their identities (personal and energetic) from each other, creating a codependency. Underneath the codependent bond is the dynamic between the wounded masculine and the wounded feminine.

Whether one identifies as male, female, or nonbinary, we all have both feminine and masculine energies and imprints within us. Our masculinity and femininity can be broken down into four aspects: the empowered masculine, the wounded masculine, the empowered feminine, and the wounded feminine. Not only do they all exist within each of us, they manifest as energy patterns in our relationships with ourselves, others, and society. On a global level, they inform how various cultures and societies treat one another as well.

Empowered masculine: This quality is protective, proactive, productive, willful, physical, strong, independent, courageous, brave, loyal, assertive, and honorable. The empowered masculine embraces sensitivity and vulnerability; it is integrated with its own feminine aspect. The empowered masculine balances the heart and the mind spiritually, valuing morals, the Divine, honor, and being just. The empowered masculine is a good steward of power and responsibility, seeking to align with rather than to dominate over. Empowered masculine energy is harnessed in the physical body.

Wounded masculine: This is the quality of fear and control that happens when the empowered masculine has been suppressed or its feminine aspects shamed. The wounded masculine flourishes in patriarchy. Parenting through the wounded masculine reinforces sociocultural norms that emotions are shameful and should be hidden. Anger builds in response to unexpressed emotions or when the wounded masculine feels threatened. In a domino effect, the wounded masculine then suppresses the feminine and oppresses others through an internal and external abuse of power. Filled with an inflated self-importance, the wounded masculine acts superior to others it perceives as less powerful or as a threat.

Empowered feminine: This quality encompasses trust, receptivity, nurturing, intuition, emotions, going with the flow, love, heart, and honoring the divine Self. It also includes sensuality, creativity, mothering, and connection to all of life. The healthy empowered feminine is completely comfortable with the spectrum of emotions, from rage to bliss. It is secure in its joy and anger. It has compassion and respect for the emotions of others but does not take them on, as it understands the gift of transformation that comes with feeling one's feelings deeply. It is in touch with its masculine aspects, which allow it to speak up, advocate, and fiercely protect when needed. It has dignity and is connected to its goddess nature.

Wounded feminine: Often a result of feminine power being suppressed, the wounded feminine is the quality of excessive caretaking at the expense of self, engaging in the victim narrative, the inability to take action on one's own behalf, and the need to ground through others. It is the part of us that shrinks and becomes submissive to domination, often repeating that pattern over and over again. It is the silent, secret-keeping, guilt-ridden part of us that develops aches and pains for the world's burdens and carries internal unrest, yet strives to please and not make waves. The wounded feminine is under perpetual threat from the wounded masculine and as a result lives in a defensive posture, enduring negative energy and behavior. The wounded feminine confuses attention (even negative) with what love really is.

The dance of the empath and the narcissist can be similar to the dance of the wounded masculine and wounded feminine. The narcissist carries patriarchal shadow qualities that suppress the feminine, mirroring the narcissist's internal suppression of their own feminine energy. Narcissists acting from the wounded masculine aren't able to connect to their healthy empowered feminine aspects and instead shame them. The narcissist sees vulnerability, a power of the second chakra, as a threat because it can lead to deeper emotions.

On an energetic level, the narcissist is living from a root chakra contraction that contributes to an arrested development in the second chakra. The contraction could be from trauma or an inherent pattern; whatever the origin, somewhere a breach in trust occurs, which prevents the narcissist from connecting deeply to themselves and their inner child (or the child they were when the trauma occurred). The wounded masculine is threatened by all the qualities of the empowered feminine. The narcissist, acting from the threatened wounded masculine, has an amplified reaction when triggered, causing them to regress and to act out in an attempt to block both people and emotions from penetrating their emotional and energetic walls.

In relationships, the wounded masculine in an active narcissist bonds (codependently) with the wounded feminine in their partner, often an empath who is not seated in their own power. Codependency occurs when both the empath and the narcissist are operating from a root chakra contraction. Neither of them will be grounded in their energetic body or their emotional center, so they bond out of fear. This unstable connection rooted in insecurity can result in an enmeshed and sometimes volatile dynamic.

When our own grounding cord is not intact, we "cord" into others, meaning that we ground through them, instead of through our own grounding cord, to find a sense of safety and belonging. On an energetic level, this faulty practice makes us vulnerable to codependent dynamics.

An empath who is disempowered — not in their center, fearing emotions, and overwhelmed by energy — is cut off from their healthy feminine and masculine aspects. This lack of connection leaves them in an ungrounded state, vulnerable to perpetuating the victim dynamic in their relationships.

While this is an underlying energetic dynamic in abusive relationships, it does not mean that the victim is responsible or should stay in the unhealthy relationship until they can own their power. Abuse is caused by the actions of the abuser and is not the victim's fault. If you are in an unsafe relationship, you must seek safety first before working on the energetic and emotional dynamics of your relationship. In the United States, you can contact the National Domestic Violence Hotline at TheHotline.org or at 800-799-SAFE (7233). You are not alone; loving volunteers and professionals are waiting with open arms to help you.

Being filled with wounded feminine energy can lead to feelings of helplessness and powerlessness. In a relationship with a narcissist, these feelings are reflections of the narcissist's disowned feminine power. Often embedded in the root chakra from childhood, they are reinforced by society, culture, and family systems.

It is important to highlight that even though we are working with masculine and feminine energy, this is not a dynamic between males and females. Again, we all carry both masculine and feminine energy regardless of our gender identity, and we all can hold both the wounded and the empowered aspects of these energies. As an example, a man could be an empath operating from the wounded feminine, and a woman could be a narcissist operating from the wounded masculine. As we heal our wounded aspects, we are able to operate more and more from our empowered masculine and feminine aspects.

Our wounded aspects are closely tied to our negative inner voices, or what we often refer to collectively as our inner critic. We criticize ourselves for expressing the healthy aspects of the masculine and feminine because they are not valued in society and are therefore unsafe to reveal. In this way, our inner critic is really trying to protect us from having consequences for expressing empowered masculine or empowered feminine energy. Because of these internalized beliefs, we also judge others for expressing empowered energies, as well as the wounded energies.

This polarizing dynamic within us is also being expressed in the collective. Power struggles, war, divisive politics, corruption, greed, segregation, bias, inequality, and injustice are all expressions of the polarities between the empowered and wounded aspects of the masculine and feminine. But while it is messy, feels painful, and stirs up sensitive issues in us as individuals and in the collective, change *is* possible.

As we embrace and embody the healthy aspects of the masculine and the feminine within ourselves, we can shift these energies in the collective. Systems and structures in society will change as the feminine draws from healthy masculine energy to rise up and speak truth to power. And the masculine can integrate with the feminine to embrace empathy and vulnerability as strengths.

Consciousness is changing, history is changing, and the empowered empath who has access to both empowered feminine and empowered masculine energies has a significant role to play in this emerging consciousness. The empath's journey to becoming empowered must include reclaiming their power in the second chakra area of the body. True vulnerability is more than just feeling feelings. While it can be a painful exploration, which gives the illusion that something is wrong, true vulnerability comes in embodying the power of the second chakra. The awareness of our vulnerability connects us with our inner child. We can even allow the inner child to act as our guide, directing us to the feelings and experiences we've been suppressing.

The Healing Power of Forgiveness

The next step after awareness on the path to empowerment is responsibility: taking ownership for the ways we have embodied and expressed the wounded aspects of the feminine and the masculine, as well as for the ways we have hurt others and ourselves. Forgiveness is a powerful tool for healing and reclaiming our power and sensitivity in the second chakra.

Forgiveness can be a trigger for many people. There are ways we have been harmed, as children and as adults. There are ways we have been treated unjustly. It takes time to work with these tender areas. You cannot authentically access forgiveness if you're still embodying anger. Forgiveness does not mean that what happened was okay or that a person is absolved of their responsibility for hurting you. It means that they no longer have power over you and they no longer take up residence in your energetic body. They no longer ground through you or cord you. Forgiveness is releasing those energetic ties and replacing them with your own energy, with love, and with your connection to Source.

Don't shame yourself if you are not ready to forgive right now. Good people can have dark feelings; they are not wrong or bad, and neither are you for having them. First, start with yourself. Forgive yourself for all the ways your wounded masculine attacked your feminine essence and made it wrong. Forgive yourself for not listening to your inner child or your intuition. Forgive yourself for ignoring your body and what your body needed at the time it was trying to get your attention. Forgive yourself for trying to be nice, and good, and proper, and perfect, when in fact you felt like a hot mess inside.

Healthy empaths are confident in their power and are not unsettled by issues that arise within relationships or in energy dynamics around them. They take responsibility for their part through self-reflection, acknowledging the need for inner forgiveness and for healing from within. Relationships are transformed through an empath's own inner transformation. In the same way, negative energy in the people around you isn't much of a problem once you become an empowered empath. When empaths are not in their power or are feeling vulnerable to tensions around them, they may need some inner element of self-care. Peace, connection, and strength come from going inward. The inner light from their center can then radiate outward to transform the energy around them. Empaths who are comfortable with their vulnerability and their emotions will be able to hold their boundaries and discern which emotions are theirs and which are other people's.

We have all experienced a dominant wounded masculine overpowering the essence of our own feminine. This experience may have come from people in your life who carry the energy of the wounded masculine, yet that voice lives inside you, too. To heal the wounds of the second chakra — in ourselves and in the collective — we are being called to give permission to the empowered feminine to rise and be treated with respect and dignity.

Feminine energy needs space to think and feel and breathe. The feminine energy within us needs space to birth a new consciousness of beauty, grace, and connectedness — the traits we most need in order to heal. The feminine will guide us to understand the essence of our divinity. The power of the feminine is centered in our core and amplifies resilience. The feminine shines the light of compassion on our shadows and invites those aspects within us that have been neglected into the light. The collective wounds of the second chakra will heal as we invite the divine feminine to dwell within us individually, connected to our innermost being.

As an empowered empath, it's time to nurture the feminine essence of your being. It's important to bring this energetic connection into your contemplative practice, prayer, and meditation. We need not be afraid of this power. The empowered empath has full access to the empowered feminine and masculine and draws on them to help heal others and the world.

JOURNALING EXERCISE

Take a moment to pause and reflect on the following questions. Journal on your responses below to help process awareness that may have arisen from this chapter:

1. Have the wounded masculine and wounded feminine played a role in your life? If so, in what ways?
2. Have the healthy masculine and healthy feminine played a role in your life? If so, how?
3. Describe you in your feminine power.
4. Describe you in your masculine power.
5. What aspect (healthy masculine or healthy feminine) do you need to give more attention to?
6. The feminine aspect of our being includes our grounding, the seat of our emotional center, patterns of codependency, the effects of the patriarchy, the wounded masculine, and the wounded feminine. How are you connecting these many dots?

Guided Meditation: Bringing the Masculine and Feminine into Balance in Your Body
Audio version available at WendyDeRosa.com/book-meditations

Take a comfortable seat and begin breathing into your belly. With every inhale, fill up with light, and with every exhale, root more deeply into your body and into the earth. Visualize or feel your grounding cord connected from your hips to the center of the earth.

Breathe here.

When you feel settled, tune in to the voice of your inner critic or monkey mind. This voice could also manifest as a feeling in your body. What qualities of your inner critic's voice come from the wounded masculine? Is the voice punishing? Is it shaming? Is it fear based? Is it doubting you? Whose voice does it remind you of? Is there someone in your family of origin who spoke the voice of the wounded masculine to you when you were growing up? Just notice the voice of the wounded masculine in your mind and in your body.

Breathe.

Now tune in to the voice of the wounded feminine. Again, it could be a voice, or it could be a feeling in the body. The feminine is less mental and more of a felt experience than the masculine. Is the wounded feminine's voice powerless? Is it guilt ridden? Is it lost, confused, overwhelmed, and/or ashamed? Is it tired and overworked? Is the wounded feminine angry but passive? Is it overcaretaking, apologetic, and giving too much? Is there someone in your family of origin who spoke the voice of the wounded feminine to you when you were growing up?

Take a moment and breathe here into how your wounded feminine operates in your body.

Now create an image or awareness of the healthy masculine. The healthy masculine may be protective, clear, honest, brave, trustworthy, strong, proactive, playful, productive, action oriented, or any other qualities that your healthy masculine shows you.

In your mind's eye, allow your healthy masculine to face your wounded masculine. Allow your wounded masculine to see and receive your healthy masculine side. See them connect.

Imagine that your healthy masculine is strong enough to radiate presence. As a result, it gets bigger, and the wounded masculine softens. As he softens, he is held by the healthy masculine, who is strong. Hold this image of your healthy masculine in your mind and in your body.

Take some deep breaths here.

Now imagine your healthy feminine. This part of you is creative, spontaneous, sensual, in tune with your feelings, and intuitive. She has a keen sense of the unseen world, emotions, and the cycles of life. This part of you is not ashamed but is rather a goddess who is regal in knowing who she is. She does not apologize for her feelings but loves herself through them.

In your mind's eye, imagine that she stands before your wounded feminine. She shines light and holds her center around her own radiance. She allows the wounded feminine in you to receive healing and to become empowered. She does not victimize the wounded feminine, who is already feeling victimized. Instead, your healthy feminine raises her up and empowers her to stand on her own two feet.

Breathe.

The wounded aspects of your masculine and feminine energy are held by the healthy aspects. As a result, they dissolve or take a back seat. In this moment, as you are breathing, allow that your healthy feminine is facing your healthy masculine. The two hold hands. They see each other. The yield to each other. They value each other. And they stand up for each other. Take a few deep breaths here and allow your healthy feminine and healthy masculine to come into balance with each other. The wounded aspects dissolve.

Breathe here.

Imagine seeing these two parts of you integrate into your body like a yin-yang symbol. The healthy masculine and healthy feminine are seen by you and acknowledged. And that is the first step to allowing them to be a part of your operating system. When the mental chatter is strong or the feeling of powerlessness takes over, remember that your healthy masculine and your healthy feminine can stand up in your body and give you what you need.

Take your time as you breathe and allow the power of your healthy feminine and your healthy masculine to balance each other.

When you're ready, you can slowly open your eyes.

CHAPTER THIRTEEN

The Third Chakra:
Access Your Solar Plexus Power

I'd like to open this chapter with a grounding practice to anchor you into your energetic body. Begin by feeling your feet on the ground. Have a sense of your grounding cord strongly anchored to your hips, dropping deep down into the earth, and expanding into the center of the earth in the form of an intricate and far-reaching root system. Take a deep breath, drawing up the essence of safety into your tailbone while declaring, "I am safe." Feel your presence in your root chakra supported by your powerful grounding cord. Bring your awareness into the throne of your second chakra and feel yourself seated there, radiating your regal divine essence.

This simple yet powerful practice for reinforcing the energetic foundation of your lower body creates stability for a balanced third chakra. For empaths, this power center is often out of balance. An empath's third chakra can become overwhelmed when struggling to manage all the energy coming its way.

The Sanskrit name for the third chakra is Manipura chakra, meaning "lustrous gem" or "jeweled city." It is often referred to as the solar plexus energy center because of its location between the navel and the diaphragm. It encompasses your digestive system, internal organs in the belly region, and your entire gut biome, including the neurotransmitters that send messages to your brain.

This chakra is the power center of personal will, identity, and ego. Governing the digestive system, the solar plexus relates to both the digestion of food and the digestion of life. As we absorb and metabolize our life experiences, we integrate them into who we are, ultimately becoming the embodied essence of our experiences. From this center, we also expand outward, manifesting our true Self, radiating our power, determining how we are going to engage in the world.

This power center helps us navigate our environment so that we can organize who we are in relation to the world around us. It is involved in our socialization and helps us find our place within our family, community, and society. In this way, we are able to connect with other like-minded people and settle into a place where we belong. However, when the third chakra is out of balance and our root system is not secure, the solar plexus region will form a false identity to attach to for survival.

Our first attachment cord as newborns is our umbilical cord. Through it we receive physical, energetic, and emotional sustenance — nutrients, bonding, nurturing, love, and life-force from our mother. This helps us regulate our bodies and creates a safe container for us to thrive within. When the umbilical cord is cut, our body redirects our system, and we rely on a new type of support coming from outside ourselves, such as food that we take in through our mouth. Our grounding cord is initially the umbilical cord connecting us to Source and keeping us rooted in the earth. Even after the physical umbilical cord is cut, the energetic bonding to the mother remains intact through holding, nursing or feeding, eye connection, voice, and the energy of love. So on an energetic level, we still ground into our mothers, as well as our fathers and other caregivers who provide ground for us.

As we grow, we experience rites of passage that help us develop a greater sense of self and our place in the world. For example, we learn to walk, we eventually go off to kindergarten, we graduate from one grade and move to the next, we learn to drive cars, we get jobs, we move on to higher education, we get married and have children, and so forth. These stages of development help us establish increasing levels of independence and personal responsibility. These rites of passage ultimately strengthen and develop our sense of self and further strengthen our ability to ground.

However, if the root chakra is contracted in childhood because of fear and lack of safety, the grounding cord underdevelops or can even become detached. As we've discussed earlier, this shifts the second chakra into a state of hypervigilance and creates an imbalance in your emotional center. The third chakra region also tries to compensate.

In a state of fear or lack of safety, the third chakra attempts to ground by attaching to people, jobs, or material objects that can create a sense of grounding. Think of it like being in freefall and grasping at anything that might help slow your fall. You can also send cords into other people's chakras when there is not enough life-force in your own chakras and your chakras are ungrounded. Other people can cord you in this way as well.

Attempting to ground through others is an unconscious effort by the energy body to create a sense of security, identity, and stability. Unfortunately, it creates the opposite effect, ultimately leading to a greater sense of ungroundedness and lack of safety.

We also commingle energy when we are intimate with people. On an energetic level, we may experience a sense of safety and security in bonding in this way and form a healthy attachment with others. However, when our outer attachments become unstable or we feel threatened, we become dysregulated, sending signals to the brain that we are not safe and triggering a fight-flight-freeze response in our nervous system.

The way that the energy body attempts to take care of itself is actually amazing. In response to a root chakra contraction, the solar plexus blows open in an effort to seek the attachment and bonding that we need to survive. However, this causes the third chakra to become overwhelmed with incoming energy and out of balance from the forward momentum of attempting to ground through others.

The imbalance caused by the overextended front side of the third chakra leaves the back side of your solar plexus shut down. This closing down cuts you off from the current of grace flowing down the back side of your energy body. This energy is essential for the health of your entire being and connects you to your true Self. When the back side of the third chakra is open and receiving life-force from the Divine, you are able to harness the energy of your personal will and fire — your confidence.

The back side of the third chakra is where we receive encouragement from the Divine. It's where we sense the Divine's hand at our back to nudge us forward into life, to give us the fire to manifest our true Self. When we allow our back body in general to be supported by the Divine and to receive light through a vertical shower of grace, we say that our Soul is *sourced*. We can shift our consciousness from the back side of the solar plexus into the center to ignite the flame in the belly. That flame is the fire for our will, our transformation, and our ability to manifest our true Self in the world. It's also our center. Our ego is an aspect of this chakra and is influenced by whether we have a connection to our back body through confidence or whether we are maneuvering through life solely via our front body.

The word *ego* can have a negative connotation — an out-of-balance ego is problematic. However, we need our ego in order to bring our gifts into this world. When you are grounded into your solar plexus power center and aligned with the Divine, you are able to embody your true Self and maintain a healthy ego. Think of your ego as the container for your personality and your gifts, the place from which you navigate the world. Through your healthy ego, you can tap into the power of your divinity to illuminate your Soul's purpose. It also fuels a deep sense of knowing in your gut. Empaths thrive with a healthy ego reinforced by a confident connection to their divine Self.

A healthy flow of power through the third chakra can be blocked by fear and doubt, triggered by negative thoughts or by unhealthy energy that has been absorbed into the front side of our solar plexus. This type of energy creates a barrier that blocks us from our power to manifest and to be seen. Such a blockage also distorts the lens you use to perceive and navigate the world around you. We call this filter the *wounded ego*.

Although the wounded ego is an aspect of our identity or the self, it stems from internalized early childhood beliefs, wounds, and unprocessed energy embedded in your first chakra. It influences your nervous system and is tethered to experiences in your childhood and family of origin. If you grew up immersed in the belief that you're not good enough, the wounded ego carries that energy. It can activate memories in your body that you are not powerful and your ability to manifest in this world is limited. Much of what we identify with in ourselves and live out in the world comes from what we have internalized and held in our root chakra. The third chakra in particular can manifest our root chakra experience, because the third chakra is a power center for our identity. You unknowingly hold this wounded-ego energy in the front side of your solar plexus, where it diminishes your sense of self, your personal power, and your healthy ego.

Empaths have three essential needs that must be met in order for them to live at their fullest potential: the infusion of support and confidence in the back body; connection with the world through the front body; and being grounded in their central channel.

It is essential for empaths to maintain balance between the back side of the third chakra and its center. When you meditate on bringing grace into your back body, you are infusing the Divine into that area. Feeling the Divine at the back side of your third chakra affirms your sense of self and your personal empowerment. It supports you to have and to hold boundaries. When your energy is congested or incoming energy is overwhelming, your essential self can be pushed out of your solar plexus, cutting you off from your source of energy and passion, clarity and direction. This can lead to procrastination, not knowing what's needed or where to start, an inability to make decisions. Fear infiltrates the area you have vacated, and you draw on false beliefs and old narratives to fill this space. It's no coincidence that indigestible energy accumulates in the energy center linked to your digestive system. When the inner fire is low, we may not be digesting food or assimilating it well; we may be stuck, overly emotional, and unable to make things happen.

An expression we use to talk about passion is "the fire in the belly." If your fire fades out, it can leave you feeling lethargic or sluggish, and it even slows digestion. The opposite is true, too. If your fire has been blazing, you might feel hyperactive or find yourself overdoing, overgiving, and overextended. You might try to control and manage situations as a way to ground or lash out at others by projecting blame and shame to distract yourself from what's happening in you. These are signals that your solar plexus is out of balance. Building your awareness that God's grace is the light that fuels the back side of the third chakra will help to balance the fire.

JOURNALING EXERCISE

After reading this chapter, take some time to respond to the following questions in your journal:

1. What new awareness do you have about your third chakra?
2. How do you experience your wounded ego?
3. How do you experience the voice of your Soul?

Guided Meditation: A Gentle Cord Cutting
Audio version available at WendyDeRosa.com/book-meditations

From your comfortable seat, take some deep breaths into your solar plexus area — your third chakra — located between your navel and your diaphragm.

This is your power center for personal power, will, self-confidence, taking action, empowerment, and manifesting your true Self in the world.

Bring your awareness to the back of your solar plexus. Place your hand on that part of your back to connect you to that area of your body. Take some deep breaths here.

You are invited to release fears about how to survive in a culture or a society that you might be holding on to in this area. These might have included some fear-based structures or expectations. Take some deep breaths into that area of your body and allow your exhales to release energy down your spine, down your tailbone, and through your grounding cord.

Breathe.

This energy that you are releasing has blocked you from trusting that your Soul came here on purpose, that you do have personal will, and that you do have a calling. Take more deep breaths into that area of your body. Release any held energy. Exhale it down your grounding cord and into the earth.

Breathe.

Then, see a waterfall of light — the light of grace — coming down your spine and your back body. Allow this light to pour into the back side of your solar plexus. Take some deep breaths and receive this light as encouragement from the Divine.

Breathe that essence of light into the center of your third chakra.

Feel the power of these words: "Yes, I can. Yes, I will. Yes, I do have a sense of myself. Yes, I feel my body."

Allow a yellow sun to emerge from your core. It's your inner radiance and inner fire. You need that fire to digest food and life. It's not overheating your body but, rather, giving you a sense of your inner light and knowing.

Let that flame of inner knowing hold your boundaries. You

are not going to be overtaken by the world in the front of your solar plexus. Take deep breaths as you allow the presence of your vibrancy and personal will to strengthen.

Breathe.

Now, from feeling your center, blow out the energy that you have absorbed into your solar plexus from the wounded ego, from your past, or from the world around you. Let that energy descend down into the earth. Let your angels dispose of it. Let the earth dissolve it. Deep breaths, exhaling, blowing out, releasing.

Now, let's turn to a very general cord clearing here. Envision all the people whom you have unconsciously corded to during times in your life when you needed to feel secure. Recite: "I'm sorry if I gave you my power and personal energy. I'm shifting the dynamic; I'm pulling my energy back. You're going to be okay, and I'm going to be okay."

Take a deep breath and pull your energy back into your third chakra. You are pulling back the energetic signals you once gave out that this was how you wanted to relate to the world. As you pull that power back, ground it down through your grounding cord. Breathe and feel your powerful grounding and sense of self.

Next, release from your third chakra anyone who has been corded into you from years of you being energetically open. Simply say, "I'm not available to be corded into anymore. I am giving your power back to you. You can ground it into your grounding cord and feel secure in yourself." Envision their energy going back to them and the space clearing between you and those people.

As you do this exercise, you may envision as many people as you'd like to change the energy dynamic with.

Take your time and breathe through the releasing.

Take responsibility for any unmet needs you have projected onto another person. Give back their unmet needs or their projections of emotions and power. Is your inner child needing something from this person that they can't fulfill? Tell your inner child you will meet those needs.

When you take responsibility for your part and release the energy of the other person that you are unconsciously holding, what remains is the shell of a cord. It no longer has charge.

Now, you can cut the cord to this dynamic. Keep in mind, this doesn't cut people out of your life if they are meant to be there. This does not sever a relationship if there is more to the relationship. This clears the dynamic of you giving your power away on an unconscious level and making space for others' energy on an unconscious level.

If you are ready, you can cut the cord using the side of your hand as if it were a blade. Allow your end of the cord to go into your grounding cord and the end of the other person's cord to go into their grounding cord. Allow them to have their light as you would have yours. (If the cord doesn't cut, there is still more to process. Wait until you know more about what the charge is between you and the other person.)

Feel your power. Feel the sun glowing in the center of your belly. It's not too big or too small. It's the perfect size for your body.

Breathe.

In that radiance is your inner protection. That glow illuminates your body, filling you up with a full presence of you.

You can complete by showering your body with light and allowing your pillar of light to be strong and radiant.

You are an embodiment of will, Self, and presence. You have the capacity to manifest your true Self into the world.

Take your time. As you are ready, you can slowly open your eyes.

CHAPTER FOURTEEN

Detox Your Energy and Repair Your Energetic Boundaries

U ntil this point, we've been working with the deeper energy layers that help you, the empath, take personal responsibility for the unconscious structures that contribute to your absorbing energy around you. Understanding your inner energy system and the patterns that have formed from wounds gives you a template for self-healing and transformation.

As a sensitive, empathic being, you are also constantly engaging with energy on the outside, in the world around you and particularly in the collective consciousness. So the energy you need to clear is sometimes on the surface. Being able to clear this energy can help you stay balanced and centered. Managing the energy on the surface is an important step in the process of empathic wellness. As you restore the intactness of your center, you will be able to manage less at the surface and to heal the deeper layers or fully repair energetic boundaries.

While the more profound goal is to develop a firm foundation in your central channel to help you hold empathic boundaries, I'm going to teach you some tools and techniques that you can use to clear outer energy and begin to repair those boundaries.

The clearing techniques described below are effective for maintenance, but they do not always shift the more embedded patterns in the body. These techniques clear energy on the peripheral layers of the energy system so that your body feels safe enough to go deeper. They may suffice when you only need a simple method or you don't have time and space to do a deeper healing in your lower chakras. They can be very helpful when used as supplemental practices *while* you are working on the deeper layers of your being.

Clearing Energy

While there are many ways to clear energy from your body, here I'm going to talk about clearing energy specifically for the purpose of repairing energetic boundaries.

Around the outside of your energy body is your auric field. Your aura is the outer protective layer, but it also carries information that relates to your Soul's essence and your inner energy. Energy from the collective or from other people engages with your aura before it reaches your physical body. For this reason, it's very important to clear your aura if you want to maintain vibrancy and healthy protection.

One way that you can cleanse your aura is through visualization, such as seeing or imagining your aura showered with brilliant light and asking any negative energy to be neutralized or to go back to its source. Another visualization is to surround your aura with a vibrant light and ask it to detox unwanted energy. If visualizing doesn't come easily, feel or sense the light. Bathing rituals such as salt baths or swimming in the ocean are very cleansing to the auric field, as is sweeping your hands through your auric field as you breathe. Sweating also purifies the aura.

When cleansing the aura or any other part of your energy body, be sure to send other people's energy back to them with blessings. It may not always be their intention to linger in your field, and it may not be your intention to linger in someone else's field; yet it happens all the time. We are social creatures, and we do need connection.

Sometimes you may just need to send someone's energy back to them so that you can think clearly, be yourself, and recalibrate your own energy. To send someone's energy back to them, you can simply set an intention (by making a mental statement or affirmation) that you would like everybody's energy to go back to them with blessings: "Thank you, and I release you. I am giving the gift of your energy back to you."

If visualizations come easily to you, you can visualize the colors, patterns, or symbols of anyone's energy that's been lingering in your aura and return it to them with blessings. It can also be helpful to see the person's energy in a bubble of light and send it out of your body. If another person's energy is invasive and it does not feel right to send it back with blessings, trust your intuition on how you would like to remove it from your energy body.

If you have also unconsciously leaked your energy to others, you can close your eyes and either set an intention or visualize that your energy is coming back into your body from anyone you have left it with. When you call your energy back to yourself, ground more deeply into your lower chakras and your sense of self.

Another simple way to clear your energy is to send the

unwanted energy through your grounding cord to compost and purify in the center of the earth. This gives the body a sense of release and renewal and transforms the energy into positive life-force.

Repairing Energetic Boundaries

Earlier in the book I explained that the pathway from your lower chakras through your grounding cord and to the center of the earth is the pathway of trust and the foundation for your sense of self. This same pathway needs to be engaged in order for your body to rebuild energetic boundaries. So take a moment right now to sense your grounding cord securing your pelvic bowl and extending down into the earth. Now, bring your grounding cord up a little bit higher to encompass your waistline. Feel secure, supported, and protected from the waist down. Take a few deep breaths and feel present in your lower three chakras. Repairing energetic boundaries begins here with the feeling of connection to yourself. As an empath you will train your body to repeat this connection over and over again.

This pathway also connects you to the *knowing sense* in the body that allows you to feel your intuition through the symptoms or responses your body gives you as signals.

I have explained the importance of becoming conscious of your aura and keeping it clear so that it serves as a boundary around your body. Once that sense is in place, another aspect of boundaries comes into play. Your body will give you physical symptoms, reactions, or intuitive responses, signals that allow you to feel your intuition. Listen to your body; it is trying to tell you something. Some refer to this sense as "gut instinct." When we override our intuition, we override our inner boundaries or our inner child's boundaries. So when repairing energetic boundaries, it's important to pay attention to your intuition as expressed through the indicators that your physical body is presenting.

If you are suddenly feeling fatigued, getting anxious, losing yourself, or noticing a headache coming on, check in with your body, your heart, and your inner sense of what you need. It may not always be clear, especially if physical and energetic toxins are present that you need to let go of. This inner knowing sense can be very kinesthetic, using strong body signals to attract your attention.

Once you have connected to your physical body and befriended your knowing sense, the unconscious ways that you have crossed your own inner boundaries for others will become clearer to you. When repairing your energetic boundaries, make a conscious choice not to abandon yourself in dynamics with others or with the world. Instead, check in with yourself and feel your grounding before you give more of yourself to anyone else. You might find that the body responds with joy and excitement. Other times, just the desire to be with this person or to go in that direction can be enough to make us feel ungrounded. In those moments it is important to recall your energy back to yourself and affirm that you are grounded into your energetic center.

When you are with another person and feel susceptible to merging your energy with theirs, engage your aura by seeing it as a bubble of light surrounding you for protection. You can also intend for a shield of light to be present in front of your lower belly, to protect the vulnerable power centers there. When you feel that you're losing your boundaries in the front of your energetic body, engage more prayer and more grace flowing through your back body. Sometimes when I feel a need for energetic support, I will ask for an angel to come to my back and hold me there with protection and connection to my divine nature.

Next, I want to address vocal boundaries. Communication is an important skill. Learning how to say yes and how to say no, or how to communicate in spite of mixed signals in your body, can take practice. Clear communication and empathy-based communication can make or break relationships.

Training in communication skills to improve relationship dynamics can be well worth the time and effort. From an energy healing perspective, verbalizing can help define boundaries for a sensitive being who was raised around nonverbal communication and messy energetic boundaries. If you were raised in such an environment, amid much confusion, it becomes doubly important for you as an adult empath to understand that you have the power to clear the air when you are confused. This means speaking the truth, even if it might hurt someone. There are ways to communicate a no without making someone feel uncared for but, at the same time, without abandoning yourself. Clearing the air for yourself through communication and cleaning up dysfunctional dynamics are very cathartic for your throat chakra and your overall wellbeing.

Over the years, people have shared with me that, despite their intention to hold boundaries, they still experienced some incursions of unwanted energy. If you undergo a sense of being blasted or energetically attacked, verbally or nonverbally, then you have every right to push back to protect your boundaries. Though your system may have gone into a fight, flight, or freeze response, pushing back will reverse the impact. If energy comes toward you from the front, you can use your hands or your intention to push the energy out. Or you can picture your boundaries like a bubble around you, above and below, front and back, and you can fill any thin areas, holes, or indentations in your auric field with your own energy.

To repair the aura after an energetic or physical attack, it's important first to ground yourself and then, using your imagination or visionary sense, literally mend any rips, dents, holes, or other impact, employing any tool that comes to you. For example, if you sense a feeling of a tear, imagine sewing it up with golden thread. If it feels like energy indented your auric field, push the indentation out, along with the energy that caused the indentation. Fill yourself with as much light as you need to hold your central channel and radiate outward. The action of pushing out with your will can clear unwanted energy from your body. It will also reaffirm your grounded personal power when someone's energy has moved you off your center and will repair your energetic boundaries from the inside out.

We are human beings, and we can't control life or the unknown. As an empath, you are not intended to figure out every single tool that can keep you safe from life itself. In fact, our intuition will walk us into the fire if there's something for us to learn through that experience; or it will guide us around the fire if there's something for us to learn that way. We build resources both by gaining tools for doing the deeper work and by learning how to navigate the repair process.

Building resources may include learning how to repair your energy body the way we just described, or it might mean reconciling pieces of your past by forgiving, by apologizing, or by developing self-compassion. Effective empathy-based communication is a powerful tool to repair conversations or whole relationships that didn't end well. We can't always prevent experiences from happening or respond quickly enough in the moment, but we can heal and return to a sense of safety when we take the time to repair or make a correction to what happened in the past.

Rebuilding Your Connection to Your Center

Connection to your center comes from a deeper underlying feeling of worth. It lies in your ability to feel the innate gifts you carry as a Soul and bring forth in the world through your healthy ego. If you have taken blow after blow to your ego, your sense of worth becomes disempowered, and you lose the willpower to bring your gifts forward.

We often can't force ourselves to believe in our own value. Uncovering and healing the core wounds that create a lack of worthiness is the first step. Next, you can tap into your inner resources, such as the third chakra area of your body. The infusion of divine grace through the back side of your third chakra brings power and confidence directly to the core essence of your being.

When we radiate from that place of knowing our center and feeling our worth, we send a signal to the universe that we value this body and this life. For example, if you enter a room that has negative or dark energy, you can radiate your presence and your love, changing the energy in the space instead of letting it consume you. That is the power of being present in your third chakra.

While I can explain this to you on a cognitive level, for you to grasp it on a level deep enough to shift energy will take a journey into the subconscious. We can do this through a guided healing, using imagery and connection into your energetic body. We've talked about how to work with energy on the periphery. We are now going to support your energy system with detoxing at a deeper level.

The intention of the deep guided meditation I have provided below is to support you in integrating the different aspects we've been exploring. It repeats some practices from the meditation in chapter 13. This longer guided practice is meant to help you connect to your inner light and allow that light to help you repair your energetic boundaries and feel your personal power.

JOURNALING EXERCISE

After reading this chapter and learning about some energy clearing techniques, take a moment and respond to the following questions:

1. What energy clearing techniques did you use from this chapter?
2. What energy clearing techniques do you find most beneficial?
3. How did you feel after cleansing your aura?
4. What did you experience when you sent others' energy back to them?
5. How did you experience energy clearing down your grounding cord?
6. Do you need to repair your energetic boundaries? If so, how did the information in the chapter help you?
7. Do you need to set vocal boundaries? If so, what would that look like?

8. What does rebuilding your energetic center look like and feel like to you?

- -

Guided Meditation: Detoxing Energy and Rebuilding Your Energetic Boundaries
Audio version available at WendyDeRosa.com/book-meditations

- -

From a comfortable seated posture, take some deep breaths and feel your feet. Feel your legs. Feel your grounding cord. Take more deep breaths and settle into the power of your two lower chakras: your root chakra, unfurled and fully present, and your second chakra, the throne where you are seated in your honor. Breathe and ground deeply.

We're going to start this process by inviting you to take responsibility for any way that you have unconsciously corded to others outside of you. Have you reached out to others from an unmet need through a cord that takes your power out of you and invests it into someone or something else? Take responsibility and pull that cord back into your third chakra. With a deep breath, draw your energy back to you. Then send that energy down into your grounding cord to strengthen your connection to the earth.

Breathe.

Take another round. Pull your energy back in from anywhere you might have unconsciously projected it out from your third chakra in order to feel safe, in order to attach and belong. It doesn't mean you won't have a relationship or attachment to those people or things. It just means you're managing your personal power and tending to pathways where you lose your energy. Pull back your projected needs and ground into your grounding cord. Strengthen your earth connection, strengthening your grounding.

Deep breaths.

Now we're going to reverse the action by releasing any energy that's hooked into you, including energy from people who are grounding into you or projecting their unmet needs onto you. Ask to release any energy on an unconscious level that is not yours to process. You don't need to make sense of it or understand it — it's not even yours to do that with. Give it back. You can send it back to the person. You may offer a prayer that it may help them ground to have their energy back. That's a gift. Or send the energy back to wherever it needs to go, to whatever its source is. You don't even need to take responsibility after you give it back. If a gentle action is needed, then you can bless the energy as you return it.

Breathe.

Now, take some deep breaths as we detox the front of your third chakra area. Envision a bubble of light with a magnet in the center. Place the bubble in front of your core area and ask the magnet to draw out any remaining energy that may not be serving you right now. It might not even be energy you're conscious of. Maybe it's collective energy. Maybe it's other people's insecurities. Maybe it's fear. Take deep breaths and keep seeing that energy move out the front of your solar plexus into the bubble of light, where it's being neutralized.

Deep breaths in. Deep exhales.

Now we're going to do another level of release in the solar plexus region. Exhale out any ego blows to this area, any time that your body took a blow to your personal will or your worth, including anything that happened in your pubescent years. Let go of energy that devalues your ability to succeed in the world or makes you afraid to put yourself out there. This can include energy you carry from the marinade that you grew up in. Keep breathing. Let the wounds release out the front of your solar plexus region.

Deep breaths.

This front side of the solar plexus holds aspects of our wounded ego. Our wounded ego is another name for our limited beliefs and the conditioning we grew up in that doesn't serve us. Some conditioning is good. But when the energy blocks our true Self from manifesting into the world, the light can't glow from the front of the solar plexus. We're going to love this part of ourselves and let go of the congestion. Tell your body, "I'm healing you. I'm letting go." You don't even have to know everything you're letting go of. It can be blobs of energy. It can be colors. It can be words. Whether it's in the solar plexus region or anywhere else in your body, we're asking to release all the imprinted wounded-ego consciousness, ego blows, pushback, fear, oppression, and other experiences where hurt people hurt you.

Deep breaths.

Let that energy go.

Let it release.

You're bigger than this. You don't need this energy anymore.

Perhaps your tolerance level for it has lowered to where you feel more of a presence of your Self in your third chakra. The bubble of light is still in front of you with the magnet. It will continue to draw out of you any energy you're willing to release on your exhales. You may also send energy down your grounding cord.

Full, potent inhales. Strong, fluid exhales.

Now bring your awareness to the back of your solar plexus. We're going to invoke the image of a beautiful, flowing waterfall of grace. You can imagine this or intend that it is there. It flows through your central channel, and it flows through your front body. But it also flows through your back body, and we're going to emphasize your back body. Lean back into that waterfall of light. Let the waterfall wash your back body and open up your consciousness that your back body connects you to a powerful inflow of prayer, grace, divinity, universal love, and life-force.

As you lean back, allow that back body to be showered off. Maybe there's muck back there or maybe shadow. As the waterfall of light washes through, you're opening up this pathway for spiritual stamina, for a strong spiritual backbone, for grace to infuse your back. It feeds the back of all your chakras, inviting you to sit more powerfully in your throne and feel supported. This back-body opening and connection tells your energy system to stop working so hard and trying to fix it all from your front body. Lean back. Allow. Receive. Replenish.

Breathe.

Now, I'd like you to imagine that a divine hand is right at the back of your solar plexus. To find it, locate the spot about two inches above your navel and mentally draw a line from there straight through to your back body. Invoke the divine hand there — the hand of your future self, the hand of an angel, the hand of God, or the hand of light, love, divinity. Feel what's right for you and allow that sense of support, even if the feeling is new.

Lean into the hand and allow it to lean into you. As you lean back a little more, allow it to hold strong, so you know that the divine hand is at your back. Maybe you didn't have this before or you couldn't feel it before because there was so much wounded projection in your history. Maybe no one said, "You are supported, and you can trust in you." This hand holding your back body silently gives you the felt messages of "I've got you, and you've got this. You can do it. Yes, you can. You can."

We'll imagine a little version of you there in the back of your third chakra receiving those messages. When you hear, "Yes, you can," imagine you are walking your consciousness, backed by the hand of the Divine or your higher Self, from your back body into your center.

In your center is a little fire pit. Take a deep breath and light that fire. It's a symbol of your inner flame. Maybe it's a campfire. Maybe it's a candle. But it's more than a match. We're going to ignite here the sustained will, your digestive fire. We're opening up the consciousness from "Yes, I can" to "Yes, I am because I will." If your fire typically is blazing, then just allow it to come down in its blaze. Let the river run beneath it to cool the earth where the fire burns. But if the fire is typically out, allow it to be lit, and know that you are your fire keeper. This is your will, your glow, your personal flame. As you breathe, you can walk around your fire, or you can dance around your fire. We're going to invite it to glow and to detox another level of energy that does not serve you, working from the inside out. From the fire in your belly, that glow is going to burn off any other energy in your body that your system can't digest.

Allow that glowing energy from the fire, the fire lit from personal will, to radiate, giving you a sense of power there. This is your healthy ego. It's good to have your healthy ego. Your healthy ego manifests your true Self in the world through your gifts, through your affect, through your voice and your actions. What you are releasing here in the front is energy that keeps you from manifesting your true Self into the world. You're letting the wounded energy be cleared out through the front.

Deep breaths. Expel the toxic energy out the front and into the bubble or, if it is releasing in a different way, just follow your body's wisdom. Now we're going to ask for that bubble of light that's collected all this energy to dissolve the energy. I like to ask angels to gather the bubble of light and take it to the Divine. If there's another image that comes to you as a way to dispose of it or transform it, please follow your wisdom.

Let the heaviness go. It's a weight you don't have to carry or digest. We're inviting more of your presence here now in the front side of your third chakra and in the center of your third chakra. See the flame you lit earlier turn into a yellow sun and radiate light.

This inner glow repairs your boundaries from the inside out. Wherever your third chakra has felt open or ripped into or leaky or torn or anything else damaging, we're going to ask for it to be repaired. Take a moment and let the glowing light from the inner flame restore your third chakra.

This innate glow is the presence of your true Self, having migrated from the divine connection in the back side into the center, where the inner fire burns. This is empowerment. We're going to give this part of you a message:

You are worthy of that fire.

You are worthy of having yourself.

You are worthy of the Divine.

You are divine.

You are worthy of being you.

Anything that has made you feel unworthy, throw it into the fire. Any beliefs you're holding about yourself that dampen your will and your worthiness, toss them into the fire. Let them transform into clear, clean light.

Now, let that flame become the size that is appropriate for your body. Not too big and not too small. You are your fire keeper. As you sit and gaze into the fire in your own belly, let the fire present to you something about your true Self, about who you really are. For example, "I am love, I am light," or something else. Let the presence of your Self in that area of your body breathe that information into your belly.

Whatever the true light of your being is, be it. Assimilate it. Let it become innate love. Let it build confidence and strength in this area of your body. Let it be something you can say yes to. Let your solar plexus and its beautiful sun illuminate, glow. The flame becomes a light in the center of your belly. You become the presence there who is solarized by this glow.

Your work as an empathic intuitive, as a sensitive being, as a human being is to not abandon the fire, not to dethrone yourself from the second chakra. It is to love yourself through a fear contraction at the root and to feel your own powerful presence from the solar plexus down through the lower half of your pillar of light. The pillar goes from the crown of the head down to your tailbone. This pathway from third chakra to second to first and into the earth is the pathway for our sense of self and access to our worth.

We have one more intentional question to ask your true Self. This question is a job for your healthy ego. The question is: "What conscious action do I need to take to support manifesting my true being in the world?" The third chakra doesn't live in the wishing, the wanting, the worrying, or the pining. The healthy ego in connection with our true Self lives in the "I am": "I am doing this. I will." What conscious actions will you take to manifest your true Self in the world and to maintain your center?

Breathe.

From here, anchor deeply into your grounding cord, into your feet. Ask for light to surround you fully and completely as your third chakra is formed by the golden sun, the personal flame you lit in your center. Your auric field radiates as your inner light shines.

The pillar of light that runs through your body glows from being sourced by the waterfall of grace. Lean back into the waterfall and allow it to come over the top of your head. Allow it to wash through your front body, releasing anything that doesn't serve you down your grounding cord. Let it go. Release

it. Then intend that this infusion of light into your central channel radiate outward, first, to the skin, then beyond your skin, allowing the auric field around you to be purified and protected.
See a beautiful purple light around the outside of your body for
protection; see that your grounding cord is supported.

As you are protected, you are maintaining the glow in the
solar plexus region and in all your chakras. Radiate from your
powerful, grounded, worthy presence.

CHAPTER FIFTEEN

How to Stop Taking On Other People's Energy

"How do I stop taking on the energy of others?" is one of the most common questions that empathic intuitives ask. The answer to this question is complex. It comes with an understanding of why your body is taking on the energy to begin with; a comprehension of both the power and the wounds held in the lower three chakras; and a knowledge of how to shift the ingrained patterns. This is deep shadow work.

To understand how to stop taking on the energy of others, we need to demystify light and dark energy, good and bad energy, high vibration and low vibration. We need to see how these polarized energies contribute to boundary issues.

In the body, when these energies are out of balance, it can indicate the need to grow in emotional maturity and emotional responsibility. You need to empower yourself by accepting your feelings instead of shaming yourself for them, avoiding them, or being disabled by them.

Emotional maturity comes from processing emotions and

taking personal responsibility for feelings as they occur. We grow and mature when we courageously face the depth of our shadow feelings, such as shame, guilt, and anger. Allowing ourselves the space and awareness to sense an emotional cycle rising and then diminishing builds our capacity to experience that feeling more fully. It fuels a deeper connection with ourselves and therefore with others. This resilience allows us to cultivate our center so that we can stay grounded and hold appropriate energetic boundaries.

Emotional responsibility means that we are aware of the difference between having an emotion and projecting an emotion. If I feel shame, for example, but instead of acknowledging my shame I blame someone else for the hurt I am feeling, I am engaging in a form of emotional projection. Having an emotion and taking responsibility for it would mean that when the emotion arises and I become aware that I want to shut down — my fight, flight, or freeze response — I stop myself and acknowledge that in this moment I'm experiencing discomfort. Before the situation goes any further, I need to pause, get clear, and breathe. Taking emotional responsibility means that I am not afraid of my own difficult feelings. I accept that it is only human to have such feelings. I'm willing to own my part in relationship struggles.

Our levels of emotional maturity and emotional responsibility determine whether we will simply sense other people's energy or we will absorb it. Emotional maturity and emotional responsibility grow when there is healthy communication and vocal boundaries are set. We can verbally take responsibility for our emotions and clear the air by acknowledging our own part in a dynamic.

In some spiritual communities, *light energy* and *dark energy* or *good vibrations* and *bad vibrations* are polarizing terms that make a person wrong for having their wounds. Yet we all have light and dark energy within us. As we get to know our own shadow, we feel less threatened by someone else's: we can have compassion for someone who is feeling pain.

The issue of how to stop taking on the energy of others raises a deeper question: In a given situation, are you taking on the energy of others, or is this an opportunity to look at aspects of your own shadow?

The second chakra work that we have done toward seating ourselves in our emotional center and allowing ourselves to have our feelings helps us to develop emotional responsibility and maturity. We can no longer blame anyone else for their shadow without looking at our own.

When we have absorbed someone else's energy, it is the power of our own emotions that is going to clear that energy. We can just allow ourselves to be fed up enough to expel the energy. Or we can pause and take a moment to tune in to ourselves. We can ask ourselves, "Am I simply absorbing this energy, or is this energy triggering unprocessed emotion inside me? Am I willing to go inward and identify the shadow issue that is stirring once again?"

Issues around a pandemic, gun violence, racial injustice, or climate change will arouse an emotional response in the collective. That's how consciousness evolves on a collective level. It doesn't come from people staying quiet and comfortable. It occurs when voices come together and express their outrage. Collective emotions and responses are part of creating movements, and you may find yourself triggered personally when faced with those responses. To hold your boundaries and not take on other people's energy, understand that collective emotions are not dark energy. And know that it is natural for you to have your own personal feelings about what is going on in the collective. By feeling those feelings and taking the time to process them, you will connect to your deeper truth.

Happiness, joy, bliss, and elation are certainly higher-vibration feelings, and shame, sadness, and anger can be lower vibrations; however, healing will not happen if we believe that the higher vibrations are "good" and the lower vibrations are "bad." True healing and transformation happen when we find our truth in both the lower-vibration emotions and the higher-vibration emotions. True empowerment comes from not defining emotions in polarizing terms: high, low, good, bad, right, wrong. Instead, your intuitive development and spiritual growth depend on your ability to embrace and feel safe processing all your emotions.

An empowered empath lives in the full spectrum of their chakra system. Even if wounds are still present, they exist side by side with the consciousness and embodiment of the self.

When you shift your inner energy, your outer world transforms. Standing in your power changes how you live in relationship with people, what you will tolerate and what you won't tolerate, where you spend your time and energy, and whom you spend your time and energy with. Essentially, you come into alignment with yourself. Who you were when you were operating from wounds in your lower energy body is not your ideal state of being. As I've been saying throughout this book, empaths need to learn how to embody their lower power centers and to courageously become whom they're meant to be rather than living out the expectations, subconscious fears, and belief systems that belong to other people.

Becoming courageous is a process. Becoming a mother

involves a nine-month gestation process before the child is born and then continues as an evolutionary process after giving birth. Similarly, being in your power in your body is an iterative process that takes time and dedication.

In our energy body, the process begins with learning to stay grounded in the lower body and present in the first three chakras while at the same time having empathy from the heart. As we transform the consciousness in the lower three chakras of the body, we shift our heart's frequency. We become more aware of self-love, divine love, and love toward others. Then our throat chakra opens up, allowing us to speak more truth and to listen more deeply. Blindfolds come off, which is another way of saying that the third eye area opens up. We have a shift in our perception, and awakening happens.

As you alter the patterns in your first, second, and third chakras, the rest of your chakra system will realign and come into balance. Your intuition becomes more embodied and clear. An empath shifts from being disempowered by energy to being empowered by sensitivity and intuition.

Having Grounded Intuition

If you are taking on energy despite grounding and embodying your lower chakras, the universe may be giving you a sign that you have a healer's gift of empathic intuition, which requires learning how to clear energy.

Being an *empathic intuitive* means that you feel energy innately through your second and third chakras. When you are embodied and connected to the power in your lower chakras, you build a sense of knowing inside yourself. In other words, claircognizance and clairsentience are working together in your system. Being an empath without the sense of knowing (claircognizance) only results in not being able to recognize what you're feeling or who else's energy you're feeling. I like to think about clairsentience as coming from the front of the lower chakras and claircognizance as being located in the back side of the lower chakras, moving through the grounding cord and the back side of the heart. Clairsentience enables you to feel energy around you and in the larger world, whereas claircognizance can be accessed when you lean back and ground into your true Self, connecting to the power of your inner knowing.

To have grounded empathic intuition, tune in to your knowing sense and check in with your intuition in your lower body. Your inner child may be an aspect of your knowing sense; connect with the inner child in your low belly. Ask your inner child how they feel about a decision you want to make or about what you may need. If the answer isn't clear, wait. Give yourself some time, be patient, go for a walk, or take a nap. Check back in with yourself later.

Empathic intuition is slower than clairvoyant intuition or clairaudient intuition. It needs time to feel things out. That being said, empaths are slow processors. They may hear or witness information and not know how to respond right away. They need time to think through or just be with the information before they can provide an answer. Fast processors tend to be more upper-chakra intuitives. They think quickly, they process quickly, they react and respond quickly, and they can make very clear decisions quickly. That's the visionary sense at work.

The visionary sense in the body relates to the sixth chakra, or the third eye. Sometimes the decisions that are being made from this sense don't include empathy or the care that might be required for connected conversations. Slow processors sit with the potential impact of a decision, and through empathy they carefully consider the whole situation. One type isn't better than the other. When both senses are balanced in you, you can receive great insights and higher knowing through your visionary sense, and you can connect to your lower body so that your decisions feel grounded.

My recommendation is that if you're a slow processor, then own it: "I am a slow processor. I will think about it and get back to you." Have that phrase in your back pocket. Slow processors need the time to check in with their body, heart, and Soul before making a decision. Honoring yourself as a slow processor is another level of embracing your empathic intuition and grounding into your intuitive abilities.

On the other hand, slow processing to the point of producing a heavy sensation or of overthinking without taking action can lead to too much density in the lower body, which can create a feeling of being stuck. In this case it can be helpful to tune in to your higher knowing by bringing your awareness to your sixth chakra, or third eye center. We receive higher guidance through the crown chakra, wisdom from our higher Self and the divine realm. This information is connected to infinite possibility, so it may be inspirational or outside of your norm. It also could be deeply connected to faith.

As mentioned earlier, the meeting place for upper-body intuition and lower-body intuition is in the heart chakra. Your heart chakra carries the culmination of love for self, others, and the Divine. The front side of the heart contains love for humanity; the back side receives love into Self and universal consciousness. The center is the light of your divinity in union with the divine Source. Your heart callings will navigate you toward the highest states of the fourth chakra, which are joy, bliss, happiness, and love. The heart will seek out life experiences that will provide those dwelling states.

As an empowered empath who is grounded in your lower body, your heart may feel clearer now. Your intuition may be telling you to learn more about your gifts and your true nature. Your heart may be calling energy out of your mind and down into this power center to listen, feel, breathe, and even grieve as it cracks open. As we heal our lower-body conditioning, the spiritual heart opens up, and we are invited to live in alignment with who we truly are. Sometimes that means changing paths, shifting relationships, and living in greater alignment with who you are *now* and what you are called to at this point in your life. The heart chakra isn't a rational place, and these callings won't always make sense to the mind, but your Soul is guiding you through your heart's intuition. Your Soul knows. Listen deeply there.

If you tend to be an upper-chakra intuitive, with an emphasis on the clairvoyant and clairaudient senses, it's important to implement grounding in your daily life. I mentioned earlier that upper-body intuitives are not always empaths. They can be powerful seers, mediums, and visionaries. Grounding upper-chakra energy through the heart and the lower body can really help information land in you through more empathy and connection.

Guided Meditation: Standing in
Your Powerful Presence

Audio version available at WendyDeRosa.com/book-meditations

This is a standing meditation. The intention is to support you with embodying energetically the key actions that help you feel strong in your legs, centered in your belly, and clear in your boundaries.

Come to a standing posture with your feet hip distance apart. Pressing your feet into the earth, feel three points: the pad beneath your first toe, the pad under your pinky toe, and your heel. As you press your feet into the earth, unlock your knees. Envision that your grounding cord is connected from your hips down your legs and into the center of the earth; at the same time, see roots growing from the soles of your feet.

As you press your feet into the earth, feel a rebound of earth energy that rises through your legs and into your pelvic floor and tailbone. Your pelvic floor very slightly lifts, and your low belly gently tones. You are not sucking in your low belly and creating pressure. Instead, you are energetically bringing aware-ness to your low belly and engaging tone there. Like a gentle spring, this action uplifts the base of your heart.

Take a deep breath in, and on your exhale allow your heart to be supported by a strong solar plexus. Let your shoulder blades slide down your back, naturally rotating your palms open and letting your hands face forward.

Your chin is parallel to the ground. You can feel the strong central channel through the middle of your body. The grace is flowing down through the crown of your head and showering down through your front body, your back body, and your central channel, creating a pillar of light.

Allow the vibrant light to radiate down your arms and your legs, increasing the presence of you in your body. Allow that ra-diance to expand to your physical skin and into your auric field. Imagine the light brightening all the way around your being, holding you in protection.

Stand in your power. Feel the power in your legs and in your feet. Feel the power contained in your lower belly and solar plexus region. Feel your heart centered in your chest. Allow the radiance from the pillar of light in your body to help you hold your inner boundaries strongly. Your boundaries come from this inner radiance.

Engage this power stance whenever you feel lost, disconnected, ungrounded, or in need of connecting with yourself as you move into the world.

CHAPTER SIXTEEN

Nurturing Your Empathic Being: Practices for Energetic Self-Care

If you continue a daily practice of centering and grounding, your natural state of being will become one in which you stay connected to your truth and your heart and are grounded into your body. More and more you'll embody being an empowered empath in the world.

As an empathic intuitive, it is critical for you to maintain a self-care routine. When your self-care lapses, sensing the energy around you can take a toll. Some types of self-care might involve physical actions: drinking more water, sitting less, moving your body, getting more sleep. Empathic intuitives are often sensitive to electronics, so keeping your computer and phone in another room while you rest can be important, too. Long baths, body treatments, massages, haircuts, and going to therapy produce positive changes in your energy state and mental outlook. Other simple self-care techniques include shifting your mindset from worry to prayer or from angst to gratitude. Reading this book and journaling are acts of self-care. Listen to your intuition and follow your body's wisdom, and you will be guided to the self-care you most need. Let your Soul speak to you through your body, your inner child, your heart, or your higher Self. Tuning in is an act of self-care in and of itself!

The rest of this chapter is devoted to specific practices that will support you in caring for yourself as an empathic intuitive.

Meditation

Many styles of meditation exist, drawn from different spiritual traditions, religions, and philosophies. Some practices are mantra based, where you repeat a mantra (a word or short phrase) verbally or in your mind; some practices involve simply sitting and allowing your mind to settle and come to stillness. Other practices include walking meditation and movement meditation. For some people who struggle with quieting the mind, I advise engaging in physical activity before meditating, to help work out the noise in the body so that stillness is possible. There's a great saying from Dr. Sukhraj Dhillon: "You should sit in meditation for twenty minutes every day — unless you're too busy; then you should sit for an hour."*

The point here is that meditation invites us to sit with ourselves and allow feelings to arise — something that's not always comfortable. Yet the work that we've covered in this book is inviting you to tune in, and that requires meditation. You are turning toward the uncomfortable and clearing that energy so that sitting with yourself becomes more doable. As with starting anything new, it may be difficult in the beginning to sit for ten minutes or twenty minutes. Start with ten

---

*   Sukhraj Dhillon, *Art of Stress-Free Living: Eastern and Western Approach* (2006; repr., New Edge Publishing, 2013), 167.

minutes a day in a seated meditation and build up to twenty minutes. It typically takes the body ten minutes to settle, so if meditating is challenging for you, be patient in those first ten minutes so the noise of the body can settle down. If sitting cross-legged is uncomfortable for you, then sit in a chair with your legs uncrossed. Close your eyes, breathe deeply, and when your mind wanders — as it will! — bring your attention back to your heart and your breath. Some practices involve aids to stilling the mind, such as noticing breathing patterns; visualizing a flame, a sun, or a horizon; or silently repeating a mantra.

I personally have a mantra-based meditation practice. I went through an initiation to receive the mantra, and I meditate with the mantra. I also implement visualizations, prayers, and breathing practices before, during, or after my meditations, depending on what I need. Finding a meditation teacher or book to support you could be a wonderful step to help you establish a daily meditation practice. And these days, the internet offers a wealth of resources, including YouTube videos that give tutorials on how to meditate.

Powerful shifts occur when you meditate daily. You find that your temperament changes, as do your responses to what occurs in life. It increases your intuition, your creativity, and your inspiration. It can also be difficult and triggering at times. Yet the more we breathe through the struggle and stay committed to our meditation practice, the more breakthroughs we have and the more powerfully we are able to feel the freedom on the other side.

I highly recommend as an empath that you find your meditation practice, whatever that may look like for you, and that you commit to doing it for forty days initially. See what transforms in your way of being as you make meditation part of your life.

Owning Your Gift as an Empath

"I am an empowered empath." Say it. Own it. Be it. Live it. This means you are tuned in to yourself and the energy around you, and you don't abandon yourself to feel that energy or take it on. Coming out of the empath closet is a big step, so to speak! When you state affirmations such as "I am an empowered empath," it's more than simply reciting the words. Feel it in your body. Ground yourself and be present in your lower chakras, just as you have been guided to in previous chapters and meditations. When you feel present and anchored in your lower body, let your whole body speak these words: "I am an empowered empath." Own it, be it, and stand in it.

Grounding Yourself

We live in a world that is chronically ungrounded. Sometimes it is because the ego of humanity is disconnected from its Soul and focused on greed or expectations of success, rather than valuing the earth itself. It can also be that we simply have more pavement, more technology, and more neuroses than ever before, keeping us in our heads and not energetically in our bodies. Being ungrounded is systemic and normal these days, yet it is detrimental to our sensitive bodies when we're seeking optimum health and wellness.

For an empowered empath, grounding becomes an every-day practice. It takes maintenance throughout the day. Connecting your energy with the earth element in your body is crucial for restoration, healing, healthy intuition, safety, mental clarity, and staying in your center.

Here are some ways to ground yourself:

- meditating
- sitting on the ground, close to the earth, and breathing
- visualizing your grounding cord connected from the sides of your hips to the center of the planet
- sleeping
- consciously slowing down your breath
- deep belly breathing
- practicing yoga
- stretching
- mindful walking or movement
- spending time in nature
- eating nutrient-dense foods and eliminating sugar

Leaning into Your Back Body: Receiving the Waterfall of Grace

Through your front body, you engage in relationships and with the world. Through meditation and introspection, you connect to your back body. As we've explored, the back body is where you connect to the flow of divinity and your Soul's consciousness. For empaths, it's a game changer to be able to tune in to the back body.

Bring your awareness to your back body and receive your waterfall of grace. Allow the light of divinity to shower through your being, to replenish you, to help you connect to yourself, to divine Source, and to your higher guidance. It can be helpful to physically lean back if you notice that your body is leaning forward. Doing so will shift you away from absorbing unconscious patterns from the front of your belly, heart, or any chakra.

Leaning into your back body, physically or as a visualization, does not mean leaning so far back that you are behind your central channel. It means focusing your awareness on your back body and feeling the light of divinity flowing through it, nourishing the back of your chakras. Be sure to ground yourself as you are leaning back. Engage your grounding cord, be aware of your central channel, and allow yourself to be showered with the light of divinity.

Allowing People to Be in Their Experience

When the front and back sides of your energy body are in balance, you have an increased awareness of when to speak and when to listen, when to act and when to wait. Essentially, you have consideration for yourself and your own energy. You are also now connected to the pipeline of divinity that runs through your body. Through the power of this grace, your spirit gains a higher awareness of the great unfolding of life.

What this means in practical terms is that you don't have to fix everything, but neither do you need to sweep everything under the rug. Receiving the waterfall of grace in your back body, with the divine hand at your back, enables you to trust that people can be in their experience without you having to take them out of it or heal them. It also opens up your prayer channel. You are able to engage in the power of prayer for an individual who might be in need.

Allowing someone to be in their experience means you let them go through their own emotional waves, let them have connection to themselves, let them have the freedom to take responsibility, and let yourself trust that the Divine is working through them, too. Empaths unconsciously help, heal, and ground everyone around them, but that's not sustainable for you or for relationships. Instead, allow others to have the experiences that they are meant to have in order to grow.

When you feel yourself getting swept into someone else's emotional tumult, pause, tune in to your back body, and visualize the waterfall of grace. If you wish, offer them a prayer, release it, and then reground your awareness in your back body.

Asking, "Is It Mine?"

Before you learned about grounding, being in the power of your lower chakras, or being engaged in your back body, it may have been difficult to know whether an energy you were experiencing was your own or someone else's. When we're not grounded in ourselves or not aware of the power in our lower and back body, we are most likely enmeshed with other people's energy through the front side of the chakras.

Now that you know what you know, you can ask yourself the question "Is this energy mine?" and perhaps get a clearer answer. Sometimes that answer comes with a feeling of relaxation or tension instead of hearing the words "yes" or "no." You can do this whenever you are questioning how you are feeling in response to energy around you. For example, if you wake up overwhelmingly exhausted after having an intense phone conversation the previous night, tune in and ask yourself, "Did I take on energy that wasn't mine?" Similarly, if you are questioning how you are feeling after engaging with energy in the collective or with others, simply ask, "Is this energy mine?"

If the answer you receive is a "no," then feel into your body, locate where you experience the energy, breathe into it, and see if there is any information about the energy you are holding. It is possible that an energy imprint within you has been activated and needs your attention in order for you to become aware of it, clear it, or release it. If an emotion surfaces as you are breathing, make space for that emotion to arise like the crest of a wave, and then permit it to dissipate as the wave descends. Emotions can move like waves, especially if we allow ourselves a good two to three minutes to breathe through the feeling. Combining your breath, awareness, and intuition can help you identify what energy is stirring in you. It can even guide you on how to work with that energy or let you know if you need further support with what you are experiencing.

Handling Projection

When someone projects their anger, blame, or shame energy toward you or you sense their unhealed energy coming in your direction, engage your grounding cord, your central channel, and your back body. Inside yourself, get bigger energetically. Visualize a shield of light in front of you and possibly a bubble of light around you. Remove yourself from the interaction and send the person's energy back to them. You can say these words out loud or to yourself: "This is not my energy. I'm giving it back to you. You can take responsibility for it and ground it into your own grounding cord. It's not mine to have, hold, or heal. I pray that God, angels, and the Divine surround you and help you take responsibility for your hurt. I ask angels to surround me in loving protection."

A conversation may be necessary, but first do what you need to do to take care of yourself. That might mean telling the person you are not able to talk until you both calm down. It can also mean letting yourself have your authentic reaction to having energy projected on you; giving yourself space to fully feel; getting fresh air; journaling; or talking out loud to a supportive friend — or even to yourself! These are just some suggestions on how you might take care of yourself before you transition to a conversation, if one is needed.

How to Be in Big Groups or Out in the World

Many empaths and sensitive people share feedback with me on how difficult it is to be in large crowds, to be around certain smells, to go to the grocery store, or to be in certain social situations. First of all, given everything that you've learned in this book, I wonder how much of your experience will change as you practice this work? It's very possible that, by engaging your central channel and your grounding, more of your Self is available to expand and take up space in your body. This will strengthen your boundaries and increase your resilience.

When you do the practices in this book, you will be more in tune with your needs, with what works for you and what doesn't work for you. You will find your tolerance has shifted. You might change the people you hang out with or discover that what you considered fun before is no longer enjoyable. You may find that going to bars, having a drink, being around smoke, and engaging in an unconscious mentality are now more hurtful than amusing, because you're removing the blindfolds to all the ways that we unconsciously mask our wounds. Your way of operating in the world may change, and how you contribute to life may change. Where you were once blinded by your own issues and wounds and therefore were complacent about how the system of the world is set up, you might now have desire to take action. You may love everybody! You just might find that what brings you joy now aligns with who you are and why you're here, and you may feel your time and energy are better spent nurturing that.

Do you still need to go to the grocery store, to work, or

to family gatherings? Probably! And you can do it. You can en-
close yourself in a bubble of protective light, surround yourself
with angels, ground yourself powerfully, build stamina in the
center of your body through your central channel, and claim
your energetic space in your body. You may also become more
capable of staying connected with yourself in relationship to
other people. When you build a relationship with yourself by
meditating and activating radiance from the center of your
being, how you show up in the world changes, and people
respond to that.

Processing Fear and the Blind Spot of White Privilege

Every one of us has subconscious fears — inherited, ancestral,
and cultural fears that could stir the feeling of shame if we
were willing to look at them. We are not aware that we operate from these subconscious fears, because they are inherent.
Subconscious fears cause us to act in ways that protect us from
feeling shame or pain. Fear-based responses may include looking away, dismissing, justifying, making excuses, going numb,
blaming, or lacking empathy. Pay attention to your fear-based
responses and challenge those fears. Ask yourself how they
serve you and whose fears they were to begin with.

Specifically, those of us who come from privilege often
have fear-based responses to energy in the world. If we've had
the privilege of choice on a survival level, then we may be
inherently operating from a fear of feeling the suffering that
nonprivileged people actually live with. Sometimes our privilege tells us that energy is negative, when it's other people's reality. For example, my husband is Costa Rican and grew up in
what the privileged Western view would consider third-world
conditions. From that Western viewpoint, his upbringing

could be seen as negative. However, the land they live on is stunning — food bearing, lush, and healing. The water is pure, as is the heart of Costa Rican culture. I've had many talks with Costa Rican friends and family who feel that Americans, in particular, are the ones who are less fortunate because they live in their heads and carry a negative or stressful energy. While the Western mind may assume people who live off the land have so little, the truth is they operate from a fullness of heart and a nurturing quality in their being. Because we haven't lived through particular struggles or overall oppression, we can become afraid of that energy and make it wrong in our minds. This is important to be aware of. When we have fear-based responses based on privilege, we can gain compassion and understanding by seeing life through other people's eyes and putting ourselves in other people's shoes.

If you come from privilege, how does seeing your life from that lens shift your capacity to be with energy that isn't yours? What comes up when you meditate on this question?

Here are some techniques and self-care practices that can support you in clearing fear-based beliefs, returning to your center, and gaining clarity on the next steps of your healing journey.

Techniques to Clear Your Own Energy

- Send other people's energy back to them by visualizing or intending for their energy to release from you and return to them. Thank the energy and let it know that you are stepping into your power and no longer need it.
- Put energy you want to clear into a bubble with a magnet in the center. Intend that the energy

should become neutralized in the bubble. Send it out to the edge of the universe to be transformed into pure, clear, clean light.

- Shower light through your body and send down to the earth any energy that isn't yours. Intend that the energy be neutralized into pure, clear, clean compost in the center of the earth.
- Cleanse the outer layers of your auric field, where energy of the collective can linger. Do this by envisioning gold light around the outside of your body, shining radiance into your auric field and neutralizing the energy.
- Take Epsom salt or sea salt baths often.
- Work with an energy healer.
- Spend time in nature, feeling all the elements: snow, sun, rain, wind.
- Listen to music, play musical instruments, or sing.
- Engage in physical movement, such as dance or running; yoga; or other forms of exercise.
- Learn pranayama (breathing) practices.
- Ask your angels to heal you in your sleep.
- Love yourself.
- Be grateful.
- Love yourself more.

Mind-Body Self-Care Methods That Clear Energy and Promote Overall Wellness

- Bodywork treatments, such as massage, acupuncture, chiropractic, or craniosacral work.
- Seeing a nutritionist to make sure you are eating in a way that supports your overall health and well-being.

- Yoga, mindful movement, dance, and exercise.
- Singing, writing, and vocal expression.
- Artistic expression.
- Swimming in the ocean or any body of water.
- Stopping to smell the flowers — literally.

Perhaps these ideas spark some inspiration for you, or maybe you have some practices of your own to add. Making changes requires implementation of a new way and dedication to following through. You are carving a new groove, making new neural pathways in your brain, when you create a new and healthy habit. So take time right now and make a list in your journal of what practices you would be willing to commit to. Perhaps there's an order you can put them in, ranging from daily to weekly to as needed. Before continuing on to the journaling exercise, take a moment to write down techniques or practices that will support you.

JOURNALING EXERCISE

Tune in to your intuition to answer these questions. You could listen to your heart, your gut, other parts of your body, your inner child, your higher Self, or your Soul — all are aspects of your intuition.

1. What kind of self-care do I need in my life?
2. What acts of self-care do I need to *do*?
3. What acts of self-care are about *being* — being more in alignment with who I am now?
4. How can I make these acts of self-care happen?
5. What structures do I need to put into place to maintain consistency?
6. What support do I need to stay on track?

CHAPTER SEVENTEEN

Thriving as an Empowered Empath

The empathic nature of every human being is waking up right now. We are waking up to the truth. We are waking up to love. We are waking up to our Soul's deeper motivation to live in unity and harmony with all beings. As you evolve through this process, you are contributing to the evolutionary shift on our planet. As you become more conscious, you are altering the consciousness on this earth.

Our social systems and structures pertaining to race, religion, class, gender, and sexual orientation are changing. Wounds and patterns that we have inherited and unconsciously acted from are now being revealed. What is revealed is to be healed. We see this through the uprising and speaking out against injustice that are becoming more and more prevalent, especially in our younger generations. Instead of interpreting what is showing up in the collective as "bad" or "wrong," how can we, as empaths who come from privilege, see that inherent shadow and suppressed aspects of humanity are surfacing and we need to make space for that uprising? As a white woman, my belief is that people of color have had limited rights for long enough. Sometimes the best way to be in your power is to hold space for someone who has lived with suppression to break through and come into their own. And empaths who have been suppressed need to connect to their inner power and truth so they can use their voice at this time to help heal these patterns and bring about necessary change.

As an empowered empath, you have a remarkable purpose and role to play right now. It may be to advocate for unity in the face of growing divisions. It may be to help reconnect communities that have become disconnected or to use your voice as a vehicle of inspiration, showing people how to connect with their individual power and purpose. Your purpose could be simply to heal yourself in this lifetime. It may be to release inherited shame and layers of fear imprints so that you shine your light and do not back down. It may be to live from the light of your true Self and embody who you are here to be.

And it's okay if you're not sure why you're here just yet. At minimum, your purpose is to become deeply connected to your Soul and find your Soul's true expression here on this earth. Keep staying the course of tuning in with yourself, listening to your heart, and asking yourself and your higher guidance for answers instead of turning to everybody else. As you continue to uncover, heal, and release patterns, your clarity will grow.

Change is happening within us and in the systems of the world as we connect with greater empathy for humanity and the planet. This is a crucial shift, as a lack of empathy has led to the injustices we are confronting today.

Having empathy means you are being touched by someone

else's experience. If you are moved to tears as you hear someone's story or witness who they are, it doesn't mean that you're taking on their energy; it simply means you're being touched. That's how we connect. We teach each other, we inspire each other, and we help each other by triggering each other. We grow through discord, and we grow by learning how to communicate instead of argue. As you practice embodying your lower chakras, you alter the energy system in your own body and hold yourself in the world in a whole new way. Feeling your higher Self, your knowing, your intuition, and your grounding allows you to have empathy from your heart for other individuals.

We empaths are so sensitive to the immense amount of pain and suffering around us that it can be difficult to separate what's happening outside of us from our own personal experience. We can't have authentic empathy if we are not whole and our deeper needs are unmet. Instead we will just get triggered regularly. Having empathy for others begins with having empathy for yourself. The most powerful way to do that is to honor your emotions and your deeper emotional needs, to embrace your feelings rather than judge yourself for having them. Having true empathy for other people without taking their suffering on yourself is possible when you gain practice with processing your own emotions. When you judge yourself, you minimize your experiences, dismiss your intuition, and make yourself small. Living as an empowered empath involves embracing all of who you are — including your emotions.

The Role of the Empath

Certain yoga traditions teach that we are presently in the consciousness of the Kali Yuga, a prophesized era of deconstruction, corruption, and egoism. And now, we are moving toward the Satya Yuga, the era of truth and living in greater unity with our etheric selves. This teaching also holds that we evolve our minds and species through the awakening, purification, and healing work that we do now, work that is leading toward a planetary shift. Personally and culturally, this healing work is not just for this day and age, but for future generations, too. For the sake of our children and our children's children, it is up to us to alter the history whose direction we now hold in our hands. We are meant to be trailblazers and to put an end to the unconscious wounding that was passed down to us. Your life is bigger than this lifetime. Let your legacy be a golden thread of integrity, truth, justice, and triumph.

As empaths we are here to touch lives by helping others to become empowered and by teaching people about the role of empathy and emotions in our spiritual evolution. Empaths can demonstrate that sensitivity is a crucial tool for connection and communication and that energy and vibration play a vital role in our mental, emotional, physical, and spiritual wellbeing.

Empaths have had to learn these truths the hard way — through experiences of oversensitivity, energetic absorption, lack of boundaries, over-responsibility, hypervigilance, putting other people's needs first, lack of a sense of self, and holding personal wounds as well as the wounds of others. The more you connect to your true light, help others to empower themselves, and live from your gifts in this lifetime, the less absorbent you will be. As an empath, you are here to model emotional responsibility, empathy, and boundaries — the very things you yourself have worked hard to gain.

You are a healer, yet being a healer doesn't always look

the same for everyone. A healer is someone who can facilitate transformation for and with another individual and who carries deep wisdom. A healer is a facilitator of the Divine into the world. As a healer, you can inspire transformation in others by being a teacher, parent, practitioner, facilitator, midwife, chef, artist, musician, and more.

The work you have done while reading this book will support you to be empowered in your lower chakras. This will allow you to have empathy without absorbing the energy of others. Through empathy and connection to the Divine, you will be able to care for the healer within you and seek out the training necessary to develop your gift as a healer.

As an empath, you have brought wounds forward from earlier in this lifetime and from past lifetimes. You moved them into the light in this life so they could be released for you and for the collective. This was a big mission, and now you have the tools to complete it. You do not have to carry those wounds anymore. You do not have to carry your family lineage of shame, sexual assault, repression, persecution, survival-based fears, addictions, or the cultural belief that you cannot be your true Self.

What you will need is a deep commitment to your center. By intimately and profoundly connecting to your Self through meditation, prayer, introspection, and intuition, you can continue to find your power in the lower power centers of your body. This is self-care for the empathic part of you. First, listen deeply to your body, your inner child, and your heart to hear your truth; then, be courageous enough to follow through on the messages you receive.

Your calling as an empath is to recognize that you are no longer a victim to other people's energy. You are here to transform your wounds, be rooted in your lower-chakra power, and bring forward a new consciousness. The invitation for you and for empaths everywhere is to embody your true Self and share your unique gifts. In doing so, you are fulfilling your role and purpose in bringing much-needed change to your community and our world. My hope and prayer are that this book has equipped and empowered you for this journey.

Guided Meditation: In Closing
Audio version available at WendyDeRosa.com/book-meditations

From a comfortable seated position, take some deep breaths as you ground yourself powerfully from your hips to the center of the earth. You have the tool of grounding now. Each time you return to this visualization, it becomes easier to ground. Know that you have the power to ground your body at any time.

Take this in: You are a powerful being here on this earth to actualize the truth of who you are. You are not your wounds nor your story. As you feed your Soul, your Soul releases the wounds and the story. As an empath, you are part of a consciousness revolution on this planet that requires every bit of your heart, integrity, courage, self-trust, and faith. Your empathic nature is your intuitive gift, and you will change people's lives with your voice, your heart, your kindness, and your advocacy. You have the power within you to make waves, not swim in toxic waters.

Remember to ground yourself. Remember to align to your pillar of light. Remember to clear your energy and radiate from the power of your presence. Use the guidance in this book to support you. Most of all, follow your intuition. It's the super-power that echoes the truth that lives within you.

When you are ready, you can open your eyes and take this new way of being into the world.

Acknowledgments

I would like to acknowledge and thank an incredible group of people who believe in me, my work, and my mission of helping as many people as possible.

To James, my partner, who is the maestro behind the scenes of our family life: I can do what I do only because you do what you do. You keep us grounded, fed, playful, loved, well taken care of, and alive with *pura vida* in our hearts. Thank you for loving me and being my major support so we may help so many people. Your mom's spirit is alive in you. She would be so proud.

To my daughter, Lucciana, and stepson, Isaac: May you always listen to your intuition, even if your dad and I have strong opinions and think we are right. We love you, we protect you, we honor you, and we trust that you will soar.

To the De Rosa and Flores families and extended families, including parents, siblings, cousins, aunts, and uncles: there are so many of you, and even if you're not quite sure what the heck Wendy is doing, you are in my heart, we are a family tree, and you mean so much to me.

Mom, you've lived through the unimaginable — you are a true empath and the spiritual backbone of our family. Thank you for raising us eight strong-minded and willful kids and for making incredible sacrifices along the way. We are your and dad's legacy.

To my dear School of Intuitive Studies team past and present — Heather, Gina, Jackie, Debra, Saori, Tony, Lynda, Ashton, Kyle, Jill Sessa and her team, the entire SheMarkets team, and all who have worked with me through the years to make this book and the school possible: We have weathered storms, rocky waters, celebrations, and growth, and this book would not exist without the collective effort and tireless hours from my magnificent team — past and present. You all deserve gold medals!

To my stunning editor and friend, Gina Vucci: Your gifts and ability to translate the depth of my work into words not only made this book possible but brought it to life. To have an editor who has done deep healing work and can understand my language is a rare gift for me and also for the reader. We are blessed to have you — who have worked alongside so many teachers, authors, and thought leaders in the field of consciousness — as a genius editor, writer, marketing guru, activist, and friend, bringing our work into the world and bringing much-needed change through your own work and advocacy. Thank you, Gina!

To Heather Carmichael, my right hand, the one who always has my back: Thank you for staying strong, lifting me up, always finding a way to the yes, and hanging in through thick and thin. Thank you for changing my life and my family's life over and over again. We are forever grateful to you, and I look forward to many more years of friendship.

To Gabby Bernstein, whose teachings, generosity, and love have been a gift to me and to this world: I adore you. I'm grateful for your friendship and inspired by your dedication to serve in the magnanimous ways that you do.

Thank you to all my clients, students, and assistants who show up to do the deeper work. We've been practicing the concepts in this book for years, and now here they are in writing. Thank you for being a part of this journey of intuition, healing, and empowerment.

To The Shift Network — Stephen Dinan, Devaa Haley Mitchell, and the entire Shift team past and present: A deep bow of honor and gratitude to you for supporting me, for sharing my work, and for making the world a better place by offering consciousness teachings all over the world. I am forever grateful to you. Also, a special thank-you to CarolAnne Robinson, my course manager at The Shift Network, for your guidance and support — for me and for so many students!

To New World Library — Marc Allen, Georgia Hughes, Kristen Cashman, Kim Corbin, Joel Prins, Tona Pearce Myers, Tracy Cunningham, and the entire team: thank you for bringing me into the New World Library family, trusting this book, feeling the inspiration, and making it possible for this work to reach so many people. Thank you to Diana Rico for your editing expertise, diligence, and grace through many iterations of the book. And thank you to Tuviel Levi at Interplay Recording and Multimedia for recording and engineering the audiobook.

To my friends across the world who have been with me in the journey of life, which has been many miles long up to this point: thank you for your dear friendship.

To all my teachers — yogis, spiritual teachers, music teachers, and teachers of life: thank you for carrying the torch and showing the way.

To my father, who "twinkles in the stars," as my daughter says: I know you are looking down on us. I understand you more now than ever before.

To God, the infinite light and the divine universe that prevail in our heartbeats, the feminine rising, and all of life: Thank you for the gift of this life. I honor you in my legacy.

And to you, the reader: Thank you for trusting me to guide you through the pages of this book. May you empower yourself, lead by example, and be who you are meant to be.

About the Author

Wendy De Rosa is an international intuitive energy healer, speaker, teacher, and author. For the past two decades she has offered education and training programs for spiritual and personal growth to thousands of people wanting to develop their intuition and experience personal transformation.

She is the founder of the School of Intuitive Studies and the Intuitive Healer Training Program & Certification. Wendy is an esteemed teacher who leads workshops and trainings globally, including programs for Mindvalley's Soulvana channel and as a top faculty member at The Shift Network.

Wendy is a contributing writer in the bestselling book *Bouncing Back: Thriving in Changing Times* with Wayne Dyer, Brian Tracy, John Assaraf, and other leaders in personal growth. Her book *Expanding Your Heart: Awakening through Four Stages of a Spiritual Opening* is an Amazon bestseller.

Wendy lives in Longmont, Colorado, with her husband, daughter, and stepson.

WendyDeRosa.com • SchoolOfIntuitiveStudies.com